Understan: the Rule of the Road

Paul Boissier

fernhurst
B O O K S

www.fernhurstbooks.co.uk

© Fernhurst Books 2003

First published 2003 by
Fernhurst Books,
Duke's Path, High Street, Arundel,
West Sussex, BN18 9AJ, United Kingdom.

British Library Cataloguing in Publication Data.
A catalogue record for this book is available
from the British Library.

ISBN 1 898660 99 9

Printed in China through World Print

Artwork by Creative Byte

Cover design by Simon Balley

Cover photo by Mark Pepper

Edited by Tim Davison and Chloe Davison

**For a free, full-colour brochure write,
phone, fax or email us:**

Fernhurst Books, Duke's Path,
High Street, Arundel, West Sussex
BN18 9AJ, United Kingdom
Phone: 01903 882277
Fax: 01903 882715
Email: sales@fernhurstbooks.co.uk
Website: www.fernhurstbooks.co.uk

Contents

Dedicated to Susie

With thanks to Captain Pete Savage, Master of OOCL SHANGHAI, who told me more than I could ever hope to know about driving a large container ship and Lieutenant Commander Ray Blair Royal Navy, who seems to have spent half of one leave period proof reading the manuscript.

1 Introduction

Not long after I joined the Royal Navy, I decided that I wanted to become a specialist navigator. I was taught by the most delightful officer, very much of the old school, who is entirely responsible for any skill in the subject that I might have subsequently retained.

One day, as we were discussing the Rule of the Road, he offered me a bit of advice drawn from his lifetime's experience of navigating warships all over the world:

'It's Indian Country out there, Paul,' he said. 'All I can say is that I wouldn't really trust any vessel that didn't have me on the bridge.'

He paused for a second or two, 'Come to think of it,' he added wistfully, 'My eyesight isn't what it was – if I was you I would treat **everyone** with suspicion.'

This isn't bad advice. There are a whole lot of very responsible people in charge of ships and boats. In fact, they are by far the majority, but that still leaves a large number of semi- or completely irresponsible ones, and if you and I are going to enjoy being on the water, it is worth while staying alert.

I have written this book as a study guide for yachtsmen. As such, its focus is on small vessels: it does not, for instance, dwell on the behaviour of big ships in a separation lane, except when it affects a yachtsman who might stray into their path. There are, it seems to me, a lot of people who derive great enjoyment from the water as a recreation, but who have never experienced the very much more difficult problems that the self-same stretch of water poses for professional seafarers in bigger, less manoeuvrable ships. I hope that I have managed to convey some sense of this in the book.

I would not wish any form of yachtsman to feel disenfranchised by this book. The term 'yacht' is used generically to mean a pleasure boat powered either by sail or motor.

I have also tried to make the format of the book as simple as possible: the recognition features first, then the manoeuvring rules. I have set out the amended 1972 COLREGs in full, with a few explanatory notes, and the book finishes with two self-test sets: the first to see how well you understand the rules, and the second, which is designed to be cut out and used for general enjoyment in the cockpit, is orientated more towards recognition.

I hope it all helps.

Years ago, when I was commanding a little diesel-powered submarine running out of Gosport, I brought her into port on a beautiful, calm, early-summer's day. It was spring tides. There was a fair old stream running east-west at the entrance to the channel by Outer Spit Buoy, and right in the middle of the channel, gently stemming the tidal stream in the light breeze, was a small sailing boat with a middle-aged couple sitting in the cockpit. I was to the south of them, rapidly being set onto the mud, and they both had their backs to me, chatting away with cups of tea in their hands.

They were not keeping any sort of a look-out. Rather unfairly, perhaps, I decided to sneak up on them. Before long, the bows of the submarine were almost overhanging the yacht – and they still had not seen me. One of my officers walked down to the bows and, clearing his throat, very politely asked them if they would mind moving to one side so we could get past. Without a shadow of embarrassment, they agreed - and so we entered harbour.

Polite as we all were, there is no escaping the fact that these people were just plain incompetent, and the sea is not a good place to be incompetent, because within a very short time you will make yourself frightened, unpopular, short of crew and possibly even get sunk. You will, in the process, almost certainly extend your knowledge of the vernacular (probably in a number of languages) and get to see some very big ships very close indeed.

Yachts can no longer expect to go to sea and behave as amateurs. UK & US waters get busier each year, with very large vessels operating at high speed, often with foreign crews who are unfamiliar with the channels. They are mixing on a daily basis with yachtsmen of every level of competence (and incompetence). One has only to see the Solent or parts of Chesapeake Bay on a busy day in mid-summer to realise just how many of us there are, and how much of a problem we can cause.

In Portsmouth Naval Base, the Royal Navy is responsible for safety in the Eastern Solent. This is one of the busiest and most restricted waterways in Europe, and it is also the centre of British yachting. Barely a week goes by in season without someone, not necessarily a yachtsman, doing something dangerous and forcing another vessel to take last-minute avoiding action. As a yachtsman myself, I enjoy being on the water for relaxation, but I recognise that I am sharing it with professional seafarers who are out there to make a living. There is room for us all, but if we are going to join in, we ought to live up to their expectations. In today's environment, you just have to be familiar with the Rule of the Road.

But things are not as bad as all that: the rules are actually quite fun when you get into them (*this is one sad hombre, I hear you say*). I hope that, in the pages that follow, I have managed to outline some of the features of the rules that are most relevant to yachtsmen without losing you to the pages of a paperback thriller somewhere along the way!

The Collision Regulations (COLREGS)

A fellow officer who joined the Royal Navy with me once explained why he had chosen a life at sea, turning his back on a lucrative career as a criminal barrister. 'Because,' he said, 'it is the last hiding place of the incurable romantic.'

He was right. The sea is the last great wilderness, wide-open and untamed. And a lot of people, amateurs and professionals alike, go to sea precisely because it is lonely, wild and exciting. When you get out of sight of land, you realise just how vast it is. The great majority of the oceans are outside territorial waters, and you might well think that we could get by without rules of any kind simply because there is so much sea and so

few ships. Besides, who on earth has the authority to enforce the rules?

In a word, we need rules because we are all creatures of habit. Commercial shipping tends to stick in unmarked marine motorways called the shipping lanes, precisely because they are the shortest distance between two ports. And yachtsmen are little better. I am told that the greatest risk of collisions between small boats occurs at published waypoints, where we all converge before speeding off to the next point on our holiday itinerary: this is a 21st century phenomenon called 'satellite-aided collisions'. Previously, if your dead reckoning was like mine, you spent half the Channel crossing trying to guess whether that bit of land over there was France or Alderney. Now navigation is so accurate that if you don't keep a good lookout you will find yourself careering uninvited into another boat's charthouse.

Most seagoing is crammed into a tiny proportion of the earth's oceans, and some areas are simply chock-full of yachts, fishermen and merchant ships all pursuing their separate agendas. We could, of course, try anarchy, but that has never worked in the past. Gradually, over the last 150 years, seamen have developed a code of rules that is widely accepted and - wait for it - actually works.

The Collision Regulations that we currently use are the result of this process. In their present form, they date back to 1972, with the addition of various amendments designed to take account of maritime developments in the world. They are 'run' by the International Maritime Organisation[1]. The IMO was set up by the United Nations in 1948 to promote safety at sea, and is committed to regulating the international maritime community. There are now 162 member states of the IMO, and it is because so many nations have signed up to the rules that they have the wide-ranging authority that they currently enjoy.

You do need to refresh your familiarity with the rules occasionally, because they develop gently with time. The long and the short of it is that if, like me, you have been going to sea since the time when Noah was still taking carpentry classes, you may still think that safe speed means stopping in half your visibility distance. If you remember learning that in a close quarters situation the two vessels are either 'privileged' or 'burdened'[2], it is time you had another look at the rules – they have changed!

---

[1] www.imo.org

[2] The 'privileged vessel', as was, is now the 'stand-on vessel'. The 'burdened vessel' is the 'give-way vessel'.

Other navigation rules (US waterways)

European yachtsmen are relatively fortunate because on the whole the Collision Regulations apply to the majority of waters that they are likely to use. Where they are modified by governments and local authorities to take account of particular conditions or circumstances, the changes are well publicised in pilot books and notices to mariners.

In the United States, the international COLREGS are supplemented by a further set of federal regulations that apply to inland waterways. These are called the Inland Navigation Rules, adopted in 1981. There are some significant differences between the two sets of rules, so the US Coast Guard has defined a set of boundaries that are shown on charts by a purple dashed line, marked 'COLREGS DEMARCATION LINE'. While the inland navigation rules have now been unified to bring them closer to the 1972 Collision Regulations, there are still a number of important differences that yachtsmen should be aware of. These are well-publicised in the US.

A third set of regulations exists in the US, governing navigation in Western Rivers and the Great Lakes[3] that has been drawn up to govern navigation in areas where there is a strong river current.

And of course there is nothing to prevent state authorities from creating a further set of regulations for internal waterways that are contained entirely within the boundaries of that single state.

Phew!

You will be glad to know that it is not my intention to dwell on the rules that apply to specific geographical areas, in Europe or the US. Regulations are well publicised locally and visiting yachtsmen, or people who are starting out on the water, would be well advised to check up on the rules that apply to their cruising area before they set out. This book will concentrate solely on the international Collision Regulations.

[3] The 'Western River' is a historical reference to the Mississippi; in the 19th century, this waterway pretty much marked the western edge of the United States' main centres of population. The Mississippi and her tributaries are included in these rules, together with a number of other inland waterways whose strong currents would make adherence to the international rules impractical.

A few things to think about on the water

It's an old military adage that time spent in reconnaissance is seldom wasted, and the best way to stay safe on the water is to understand how the other guy is thinking. Accordingly, before we start on the rules themselves, I thought it might be worth taking a few moments to have a look at the difficulties confronting the skipper in the other ship, boat or fishing vessel.

Merchant ships

Recreational yachtsmen are just one of the many problems that the deck officer of a large ship has to deal with. Despite this, I have found the great majority to be extremely professional in their conduct towards us. There comes a time, however, when the ship is surrounded by so many small boats – take the Solent in mid-summer, for instance – when he has no option but to plough carefully on and let yachtsmen, in their vastly more manoeuvrable craft, flow around him.

On the high seas there will be times when a big ship quite simply will not notice you. Many merchant ships have no more than a couple of people on the bridge at sea. The deck officer's job is to navigate and run the ship. He will sometimes have to operate the ship's radios – and he is also responsible for collision avoidance. If he is putting a fix on the chart, and his lookout just happens to be tying up his shoelaces, polishing his spectacles or just dreaming about that delightful creature he met last month in Buenos Aires, there is not a whole lot that the ship will be able to do to keep out of your way. Under these circumstances, ploughing on regardless and putting your faith in the Rules of the Road will make you feel wonderfully righteous, but may not prevent you from getting wet.

In inshore waters, nearly all big ships carry a pilot with local knowledge to supplement the bridge team. Because of this, and because the waters are busier, the standard of lookout is likely to be pretty good. However, the effect of this is more than offset by the manoeuvring limitations imposed by shallow water. Just consider their draught. A large vessel can draw 50 ft (15 m) or more. When you have a moment, take a pencil and draw out the available water for vessels of this size on a chart of your normal cruising ground, and compare it with the amount of water available for a small yacht. But that's not his only problem: tidal streams may be stronger and more variable close inshore, and proximity to the bottom reduces the effectiveness of a ship's rudders and propellers. So, not only does

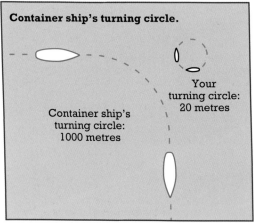

Container ship's turning circle.

Your
turning circle:
20 metres

Container ship's
turning circle:
1000 metres

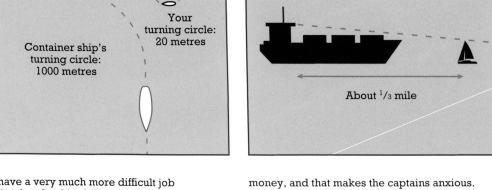

Bow blanking

About ⅓ mile

he have a very much more difficult job navigating, but his ability to turn or stop may be less than it would be in deep water. And guess what – that's precisely where he finds the greatest concentrations of yachtsmen.

As if this was not enough, if you get in front of a big merchant ship there is a chance that you will be hidden behind the bow, or a great row of containers on the upper deck. According to the skipper of a large container ship that I visited recently, a fully loaded container ship may be completely blind for something like ⅓ of a mile ahead. If he alters course, his turning diameter is something in the region of half a mile – compared to a yacht's 20-odd metres, and he only has to roll by 5° to increase his draught by 2 metres because of the rectangular section of the ship's hull. Since a large ship will often allow only a couple of metres as its under-hull clearance when entering harbour, it will quite simply go aground if too much rudder is used.

Nor can the ship stop easily. If the Captain was to put the engine controls full astern at 12 knots, the flow of water over the propellor and torque limitations would prevent the shaft from even turning in reverse until the ship's speed had reduced to 7 knots. Thereafter, it would take up to 1 mile to come to a halt. It is no wonder that many of them just plough on regardless. There is often not much more that they can do.

Finally, I have yet to come across any merchant ship that isn't working to an impossibly tight deadline. These are people who rigidly apply the rule that the least distance between two points is a straight line (or a great circle when they are doing long ocean passages) and they stick to it. Well-regulated shipping lines plan the ships' voyages half-way round the world to the nearest 6 minutes: asking them to slow down or to stray too far from their track costs their owners

money, and that makes the captains anxious.

Under the circumstances, big merchant ships do pretty well. But a colleague of mine in the Army once told me an ancient operational saying of his regiment: something to the effect that *'An assumption is the mother of a foul-up'*. If you are prepared to assume that a big ship will always see you and take appropriate avoiding action, you are a braver person than I am. On the other hand, if you can think ahead and make some small alteration at an early stage that prevents them from having to worry about you at all, you will be spreading sunshine and happiness wherever you go. This really is not too difficult to do, provided you take the action early enough: normally a gentle alteration of course or speed at the outset will significantly increase your passing distance.

Fishing boats

Fishing boats are a different problem altogether, but they are often equally constrained. Even if you can't see any nets or lines, you can generally tell whether a boat is actually fishing by its speed. Most fishing is conducted at very low speeds (5 knots or less), which puts them on a par with a sailing boat. By contrast, when moving between fishing areas or coming home, they go like the clappers.

Just think of the skipper for a moment. He's out there day and night, gale or calm, trying to earn an honest crust to feed his family. His boat will almost certainly be connected to an impossibly complex underwater structure consisting of wire, cordage and live fish, which is valuable, unmanoeuvrable and potentially very dangerous. The tension on trawl wires is measured in tons, and fishing boats often work in close proximity to wrecks and bottom obstructions. This is a demanding, tough environment, very different from that enjoyed by pleasure-boat sailors. It is only fair that we give them a good offing and do everything possible to avoid running over their wires or making them alter course for us.

If you are cruising away from your home waters, it's often worth looking up the characteristics of local fishing activity in the Admiralty Pilot or some other reliable reference book. I was once badly caught out while making a dived submarine passage through the Mediterranean. It was night time and I started seeing a succession of flashing white lights through the periscope that were passing down each side of the boat at a range of about half a mile. Then they started getting closer, and it suddenly occurred to me that I was swimming gently into a large, static fishing net. Happily, I was in time to reverse course without snagging the nets, and escaped with little more than a bit of dented pride. The next morning when I consulted the Admiralty Pilot for the area I found it was all there, written up in black and white, and a little research in advance would have saved me from getting into that position in the first place.

Warships

That brings me to the subject of warships. Warships are generally well-manned and keep a more-or-less reliable lookout. But they are also extremely unpredictable. Warships manoeuvre, turn, speed up and slow down to a rhythm of their own. They won't want you to get too close, even when they are at anchor, and they will very often tow things in the water with no obvious signals at all. More than that, they can get quite intimidating. I once got too close to a nuclear submarine off the entrance to Plymouth and was very properly given a stern warning by an escorting frigate, who invited me in no uncertain terms to reverse course and keep out of the way. My very strong advice is to stay clear at all times, particularly if they are doing obviously difficult manoeuvres: launching aircraft, replenishing at sea or firing weapons.

Yachtsmen

Let me finally talk about the most unpredictable person of all: the yachtsman. Many have done no formal training before launching themselves onto the water. Few have a detailed knowledge of the Rules of the Road. Armed only with arcane inter-pretations of obscure rules, they will plough on regardless, expecting everyone else to give way. By all means, invite them on board for supper when you reach your destination, offer them a drink and have a laugh. But always keep a wary eye on them at sea, and be prepared for their look-out to be – how can I say this – less than perfect.

What you can do to make things easier

So if that has not put you off going to sea, I suppose nothing will. What then can we do to make things a little easier and safer for ourselves?

Take action early. The one thing that I have learned during a lifetime at sea is that one should treat all other seafarers with respect, no matter what vessels they are out there in. Stay alert. Where it is possible to do so, take early action to prevent a close quarters situation from developing: often all it takes is a gentle alteration of course or speed in good time and the whole problem goes away. But remember: the other ship will probably be able to see a large alteration of course, but it won't find it anything like so easy to know that you have increased or reduced your speed by a few knots. If you are trying to let him know that you have the situation under control, you need to make the alteration noticeable and make it good and early.

Keep a good lookout. There is a lovely passage in a book about whaling that I read long ago. The doctor and the first mate of a whaling factory ship were standing on the bridge wing during a passage south when they see an albatross coming towards them on the starboard bow. The albatross was gliding effortlessly over the surface of the water. They watched it approach from about a mile off, making only the smallest of movements to prevent its wingtips from clipping the waves. It passed close down the starboard side without diverging from its path, or reacting to the ship in any way. Eventually, it disappeared from sight astern. As it faded from sight, the doctor turned to his companion and said: 'Do you know, I would swear that it hasn't even noticed we were here.'

Ladies and gentlemen, don't be an albatross! They can swim better than you can. I never cease to be amazed by how badly some of my fellow yachtsmen keep their lookouts.

No matter whether you have radar, or any amount of other gadgets onboard, your most sensitive anti-collision device, in reasonable visibility at least, is the old-fashioned eyeball! Use it. On a cold night watch, it is tempting to hunker down in the cockpit or the wheelhouse, but it is amazing how quickly a ship can bounce out of a clear horizon to frighten you if you are not looking out. Make sure that you regularly look behind the genoa, and astern, and round the back of any bits of structure that may obstruct your view. Just by standing up, you can often significantly extend your horizon range, particularly in a swell. There is no rocket science about this: it is quite simply good seamanship to keep a rigorous lookout.

Make sure that you do everything you can to be seen. Make it easier for other ships. Use the right lights and shapes; check that your lights are working when you switch them on. Get a radar reflector.

And finally, if you are worried about a ship getting too close, you can always call him up on VHF Channel 16 and ask him what his intentions are. (VHF Channel 13 is the working bridge-to-bridge communications frequency.)

Checking bearing movement

The No 1 life skill for yachtsmen, and indeed all seafarers, is the ability to work out whether a risk of collision exists. This is very simple: risk of collision exists when you are closing another ship on a steady or near-steady bearing. If you both remain on a steady bearing and the range is decreasing you will, in time, hit each other. If the bearing is moving, left or right, you will not collide.

So you have to be able to determine whether the bearing of another ship is steady or moving.

In a big ship with a stabilised gyro compass, this is a relatively simple matter. In a small yacht, bouncing around in a heavy swell, it is something of an art form.

The obvious solution is to use a hand-bearing compass but anyone who has ever tried to use one in a motor boat doing 25 knots, or a close-hauled sailing boat, will know that the result is something of a lottery. It may be possible, and I would strongly recommend taking 3 or 4 readings at once and averaging them. Even then you will be lucky to get an accuracy of less than 2 – 3 degrees, and this is not accurate enough to tell whether a ship some distance away is moving left or right.

A compass-stabilised radar can sometimes help give an appreciation of bearing movement, but the small scanner size of most yachts' radars will often produce a bearing accuracy of 2 – 3 degrees as well, and it is generally not very reliable.

A more sensible solution is to check the ship's movement against the background[5]. In general, you can consider the background, if sufficiently distant, to be on a more-or-less steady bearing. Watch the other vessel and see if it is moving

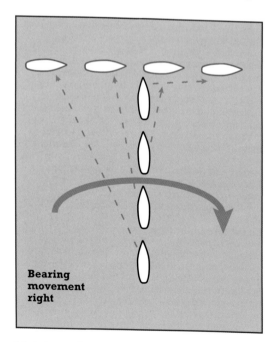

Bearing movement right

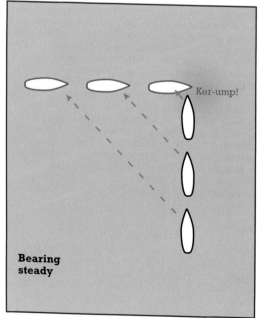

Ker-ump!

Bearing steady

[5] In fact, you will find that your brain does this subconsciously. You just have to recognise it and make sure that you use the information properly.

I have frequently read advice that you can check bearing movement against a fixed part of the boat's structure (like a guardrail stanchion). This gives you relative bearing, not true bearing, and is only as accurate as your ability to steer a perfectly straight course. In my view, it is less accurate than a handbearing compass and I would always rather use a distant object for comparison.

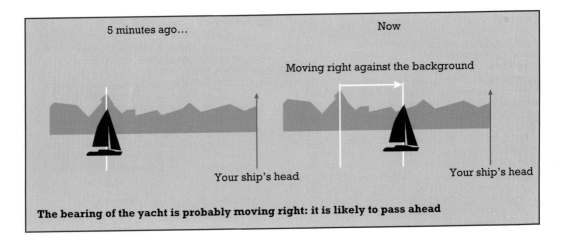

5 minutes ago...   Now

Moving right against the background

Your ship's head   Your ship's head

The bearing of the yacht is probably moving right: it is likely to pass ahead

across the background: it will either be moving right, left or remain steady. This is a pretty good indicator of absolute bearing movement.

Don't take it as gospel truth, though: merely use it as an indicator. Clouds drift across the sky, and land will probably have a gentle bearing movement one way or another as you sail past it: you will need to take this into account. However, if you are sensible, you may well find this a good way of checking another vessel's bearing movement from a yacht. Anyway, experiment with it and see if it works for you.

Having said this, I have to admit that I once almost embarrassed myself in the Straits of Dover by taking bearings of the stern of a ship I was passing at quite close range. The bearing of the stern was moving steadily right. It was only when I got really close that I realised her bow was beginning to move left. Some-where in between, my logic told me, there must be a part of the ship that was on a steady bearing, and if I did not do something dramatic, I would hit it.

The moral is this: at close quarters, you must make sure that all bits of a ship, and anything that she might be towing, are all moving in the same direction! This is quite important.

As a yachtsman, the thing to remember is that you have a very much more manoeuvrable boat than most other seagoers. You have no deadlines of great importance to keep, and you should be able to keep out of peoples' way relatively easily. So why stress yourself?

Radar

More and more of us are buying radar sets for our boats; personally, I thoroughly approve of this (although, as it happens, I don't own one myself). But whatever you do, don't become a slave to it. There are three reasons for this: firstly your eyes, properly applied, are better than any radar set ever invented in good visibility. Secondly, after about 5 minutes, looking at a radar set is enough to send anyone to sleep. Thirdly, that's not what you go boating for.

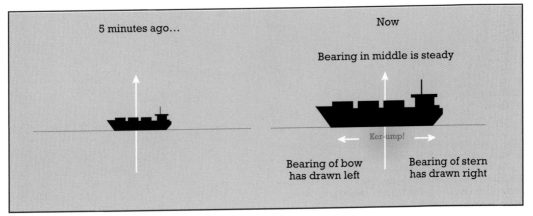

5 minutes ago...   Now

Bearing in middle is steady

Ker-ump!

Bearing of bow   Bearing of stern
has drawn left   has drawn right

Use radar as a tool when you need it. Use it in restricted visibility (when it is pretty much essential), with one person watching the screen and another acting as eyes and ears above deck. Use it for checking the range of land, or another ship when you need confirmation (although I don't imagine that this will be very often). And use it when you are uncertain of your navigation.

I would be very surprised if you need to keep it on the whole time, though – even warships go for sometimes quite extended periods with radar switched off, and submarines almost never use it. The problem is that it is a bit like a TV set switched on in the corner of the room: your eyes are always drawn to it, and after a while it becomes a comfort blanket[6]. But it is also a bit of an illusion: it does not pick up every contact, nor does it make collision avoidance particularly easy. And of course, it uses a lot of battery power if you are on a sailing boat.

Mnemonics

Finally, I would just say by way of introduction that this book is riddled with my personal mnemonics. Some, you will no doubt say, are facile. That's OK: it's just the way that my brain is wired up. Use mine or think of your own. It doesn't matter, but in my experience this is a subject that really lends itself to the use of mnemonics, and sometimes they just make you laugh – and when you can laugh about one of the Rules of the Road, it is probably fixed in your brain. I make no apologies for this. Enjoy it.

And the final word ...

Actually, there are two final words, and they are what some of the big-ship drivers call us yachtsmen.

WAFI   Wind-assisted total idiot
PAFI   Power-assisted total idiot

Don't be one: drive your boat with consideration for other seafarers!

'Under way' and 'making way'

People sometimes get confused between these two.

'Under way' refers to a vessel that is not at anchor, or made fast to the shore, or aground.

'Making way' refers to a vessel that is moving through the water.

---

[6] We all get dependent on electronics: if I asked you to sail for a whole season without switching on your GPS set, would you be happy to do so? I suspect the majority of us would not, yet only 10 years ago we were relying on Decca, and 10 years before that the majority of yachtsmen were going along on DR and EP.

2 How to recognise other vessels: lights & shapes

One of the early cookery books[1] started off a recipe for jugged hare with the eminently sensible instruction: 'First catch your hare'. Good advice. The Collision Regulations are partly dictated by the relative manoeuvrability of the two vessels involved, for which identification of the other ship is vital. So before we start it is worth taking a bit of time to think about how you recognise other vessels. First we will look at lights and shapes, and then we will delve into the murky world of sound signals.

In daylight, recognition of vessels is often relatively simple. A fishing vessel looks like – well a fishing vessel, actually. And a dredger is pretty much unmistakable. But are those two merchant vessels following closely behind each other part of a tow, or are they just good friends? And is that ship over there free to manoeuvre or could it be constrained by its draught? To help you find out, the rules prescribe a set of daytime shapes that will let you know if there is something unusual about a vessel, and when it cannot manoeuvre as well as you might expect.

At night, or in restricted visibility, just about all vessels show **sidelights** and a **stern light**. In addition, the majority will show one or two masthead **steaming lights**. These lights tell you that there is someone out there, and help you determine the range, size and aspect of the other vessel.

But they won't tell you if there is something unusual about it. Vessels with limited manoeuvrability use a set of supplementary navigation lights that will tell you what it is, and in broad terms where its limitations lie. For the purposes of this book, I have called these the 'identification lights'. They may or may not be displayed with side, stern or steaming lights, depending on the vessel and its circumstances.

> **IMPORTANT**
> Do remember that lights and shapes are always exaggerated in books like this. Very often they will be very much more difficult to see, or obscured against the background. Sometimes, they just won't be there at all. So stay flexible!

The fundamental assumption behind the Collision Regulations is that only power driven vessels have complete freedom of manoeuvre (unless they are not under command, restricted in their ability to manoeuvre, etc). Every other sort of vessel, by implication, is constrained to some degree. It follows that power driven vessels do not, as a matter of course, show identification lights or shapes, whereas most other vessels do so.

> **When lights & shapes must be used (Rule 20)**
>
> **Lights are to be shown:**
> - From sunset to sunrise
> - From sunrise to sunset, in restricted visibility
> - Whenever the skipper thinks it necessary
>
> **Shapes are to be shown by day**
>
> *Lights and shapes are there to inform other vessels of what you are up to.*
> *If you think that showing them will help other people, then do so.*
> *At night, the only other lights that you are allowed to show are those that cannot be mistaken for a navigation light.*

[1] For those of you with a culinary bent, this is attributed to one Mrs Glasse, who wrote in the 18th century. It would be interesting to know how she handled Angels on Horseback, or Fairy Toast.

Navigation lights

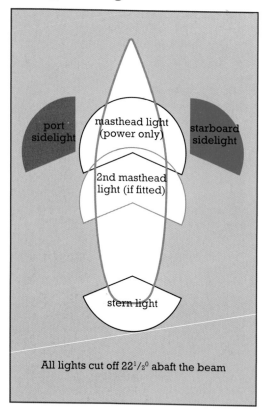

All lights cut off $22^1/_2^0$ abaft the beam

Side and stern lights

Side and stern lights , between them, cover the full 360 degrees of arc, and their purpose is to allow you to estimate the orientation of the other vessel[2]. They are *universally displayed by vessels under way* at night or in restricted visibility, with only a very few minor exceptions, detailed later in this section.

The port and starboard navigation lights extend from the bow to the cut-in of the stern light, 22.5 degrees abaft the respective beam, and the stern light covers the rear sector, from 22.5 degrees abaft each beam, through the stern.

Coincidentally, these arcs are designed so that,

if you are closing another vessel from within the arc of his stern light, by day or by night, you are officially the overtaking vessel, with all the obligations that that brings (Rule 13b).

> *The colours of side lights are not difficult to remember:*
>
> *'Left' has 4 letters, so does 'Port'.*
> *Port wine is red, so is the port hand light.*
>
> *That leaves 'Right',*
> *'Starboard and 'Green' by default.*

Masthead steaming lights

Steaming lights are white lights carried at, or close to, the masthead, with arcs of visibility extending through the bow back to 22.5 degrees abaft each beam. In other words, the arc is precisely that of the two side lights combined.

Power driven vessels generally carry two steaming lights, the after one discernibly higher than the forward one. However, if the vessel is shorter than 50 metres in length, it may carry only one.

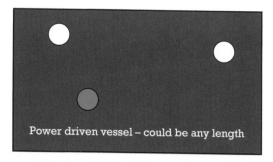

Power driven vessel – could be any length

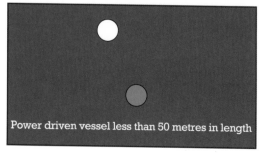

Power driven vessel less than 50 metres in length

[2] It is worth checking your own navigation lights periodically:
  • Make sure they work
  • Check that you carry spare bulbs
  • Check that the arcs are not obscured by obstructions (eg liferafts)
  • Check that the cut-offs are clean and that there is minimal cross-over.

Masthead steaming lights are shown by nearly all power driven vessels under way.

They are also shown by sailing vessels operating under power only, but not when they are sailing (if you are sailing, you are not 'steaming').

There are a few categories of power driven vessels (eg vessels Not Under Command[3]) that do not show steaming lights. Nor do vessels being towed (which are not under their own power, and therefore not 'steaming'), although they do carry side and stern lights when making way to let you know that they are there.

Identification Lights

Side lights and steaming lights are sectored. Identification lights, on the other hand, are generally visible around 360 degrees of horizon so people approaching from any angle can see what is going on (towing lights are probably the only exception to this). They also tend to be located below the steaming lights and above the side and stern lights.

A few tips about identifying vessels' lights:

- *Always start by looking for the sidelights and masthead steaming lights – this will give you the size, range and orientation of the other vessel. Once you have sorted them out, look for the identification lights to tell you what the ship is doing.*

- *Identification of vessels at night is seldom easy, particularly if you are new to it. Most vessels do actually carry the proscribed lights and shapes, but they are often difficult to see, and frequently they get lost among other lights. Liners, for instance, are often lit up like Christmas trees, and many fishing vessels have extremely powerful working lights shining out from the stern which can completely drown the navigation lights.*
- *Sometimes you will lose a small vessel against a well-lit background, like a town or a sea front.*
- *Always try to identify a ship early, using binoculars where appropriate, and make sure that you keep a good lookout, particularly at night.*

I will divide the next section into four parts:

- The most familiar lights. These are the ones carried by vessels that are least impaired in their ability to manoeuvre (power driven and sailing vessels, tows, pilot vessels and fishing boats).
- The more constrained categories of vessel (Restricted in their Ability to Manoeuvre, Not Under Command).
- Those vessels that simply cannot manoeuvre at all (anchored and aground).
- A few oddballs that you might see from time to time.

[3]*'Not under command, no steaming lights found.'*
Well, it works if you have a particular kind of accent, and your hearing's not too good.

The most familiar vessels

Power driven vessel when under way

Shapes	None.
Identification lights	None.
Side and stern lights	Yes – when under way 2 masthead lights, the after one higher than the forward. Vessels less than 50 m in length may show 1 masthead light.
Masthead steaming lights	Yes – when under way.
Small vessels	A vessel of less than 12 m in length may, instead of the above lights, show an all-round white light and sidelights. A vessel of less than 7m in length whose speed does not exceed 7 knots may, instead of the above lights, show a white all-round light. Additional sidelights are recommended, but not obligatory.

Under 50 m

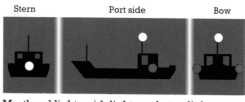

Masthead light – sidelights and sternlight.

Under 12 m

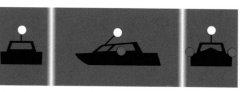

May show all-round white light (instead of masthead light and sternlight) + sidelights.

These lights are shown whether a vessel is making way or not – provided that she is under way (ie not at anchor, made fast to the shore or aground).

A sailing vessel operating her engine – whether she has sails raised or not – is expected to manoeuvre as an unencumbered power driven vessel. This may entail gybing in a heavy wind, and could require a little forethought in difficult conditions.

Over 50 m (obligatory) **Under 50 m** (optional)

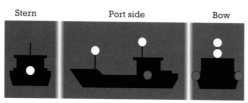

Masthead light – second masthead light aft and higher – sidelights – sternlight. Second masthead light is optional for vessels less than 50 m.

Sailing boats

Shapes	None: a sailing boat needs no additional identification by day. When the engine is being used as well as sails, a cone apex downwards is shown forward, where it can best be seen.	**Side and stern lights** — Side lights and stern light when under way (ie even when stopped in the water). Vessels less than 20 m in length can amalgamate these into a single combined lantern (with the same colours over the same arcs). This is shown at the masthead, but NOT when the engine is being used for propulsion.
Identification lights	A red all-round light over a green all-round light is optional for sailing vessels.	

▶

Vessels less than 7 m in length should show side and stern lights if they can. If not, they should have a white torch of sufficient strength to help it avoid a collision.

By day: sailing vessels using their engines for propulsion but with sails hoisted should show forward a cone, point down.

Masthead steaming lights None.
Except when the engine is being used, in which case standard lights for a power driven vessel.

Only a very few sailing boats carry the two all-round lights at the masthead. It should in any case never be used when a combined lantern is shown at the masthead.

'Red over green gets your sailing boat seen.'
Same colour scheme as traffic lights.

Most sailing vessels make do with sidelights and a stern light. And the majority of yachtsmen (ie those with sailing boats less than 20 m in length) are allowed to combine these into a single 'combined' masthead light.

Stern   Port side   Bow

Sidelights & sternlight only – no masthead light

Under 20 m may have combined masthead lantern (red/green/white) with no other lights.

From the bridge of a ship, yachts are never easy to detect. Their lights are weaker than other vessels. Quite often they are wooded by obstructions (liferafts on the stern rails are a prime culprit) and sometimes they just go out. However, they are better than nothing. For that reason, if you have a boat of less than 7 m in length and sail it at night, you should if at all possible fit proper navigation lights. Don't rely on a white torch to do anything other than alert someone to the fact that you are there: a ship may not detect a boat this small on radar and the responsibility of avoiding a collision will rest exclusively with you.

(Rare) A yacht may carry an all-round red over green, plus side and stern lights.

When you start using your engine, you should change to a steaming light, side lights and a stern light. I have sometimes seen boats sailing around with the combined lantern over the steaming light – it looks pretty silly.

Personally, I have never confused the cone apex downwards (a sailing boat propelled by machinery) with the cone apex upwards (a fishing boat with outlying gear extending more than 150 m).
If you wanted a mnemonic, I suggest that the cone apex downwards looks a bit like the underwater hull shape of a sailing boat. Drive over someone's fishing gear and you may find yourself capsized (apex upwards).

A sailing yacht when motor sailing shows the same lights as a power vessel. So engine on, masthead lights on.

Vessels engaged in fishing (other than trawling)

Shapes	2 cones, apex together, in a vertical line one above the other. A cone apex up in the direction of outlying gear when that gear extends more than 150 metres away from the boat.
Identification lights	Red all-round light above a white all-round light. All-round white light in the direction of outlying gear when that gear extends more than 150 metres away from the boat.
Side and stern lights	Side and stern lights, only when making way through the water.
Masthead steaming lights	None.

Stern   Starboard side   Bow

All-round red over white lights, plus sidelights and sternlight (if making way).When outlying gear extends more than 150 metres all-round white light (or, by day, a cone - point up) in the direction of the gear.

By day: trawlers and fishing vessels show a shape consisting of two cones with their points together.

Gear extending more than 150 m.

There are two criteria to be a 'Vessel engaged in fishing': you have to be fishing, and your fishing gear should be such that it makes manoeuvring difficult. You don't suddenly get to qualify when you put a mackerel spinner over the stern of your boat!

Fishing boats do not show a steaming light, although trawlers generally do. When stopped, neither shows sidelights. In practice, the identifying lights of a fishing boat or trawler will be dwarfed in intensity by the working lights. The working deck is nearly always floodlit at night, and from a distance fishing boats will often be distinguishable by these intense white lights, far brighter than the navigation lights. They are often manoeuvring at slow speed, and quite often work in fleets.

Fishing and trawling shapes are pretty unnecessary, in my view. By day there is almost no mistaking a fishing vessel, and they may carry the shapes whether actually engaged in fishing or not. However, you should pay attention to the upward-pointing cone, if you see it, and pass on the other side of the boat.

I remember the lights of a vessel engaged in fishing as a red mullet lying on a bed of ice in the hold. The trawler has been less successful. It has only managed to drag up some green seaweed from the seabed to put on the ice.

The fishing shape – two cones joined at the apex – is like a child's representation of a fish (or, in my case, an adult's)

Don't be fooled by the rule that says that these lights and shapes should only be shown by vessels that are actually fishing (Rule 26e). You will often see boats tied up in harbour still showing their fishing shapes, and occasionally even their fishing or trawling lights.

Vessels engaged in trawling

Shapes	2 cones, apex together, in a vertical line one above the other.
Identification lights	Green all-round light above a white all-round light.
Side and stern lights	Side and stern lights, but only when making way through the water.
Masthead steaming lights	A masthead light behind and above the green fishing light: obligatory for fishing vessels greater than 50 m in length, and optional for smaller vessels.

Stern	Starboard side	Bow

Vessels trawling (ie towing some kind of net): all-round green over white lights. Show regular navigation lights when making way, but not when stopped.

Trawlers are the most common form of fishing vessel that you will see in UK waters. Like more general fishing vessels, their lights will often be eclipsed by the working lights. Give them as much clearance as you can: when hauling in their catch, their nets often lie on the surface up to 150 metres astern.

If you find yourself in the middle of a fishing fleet, don't panic - even though this usually happens at about 0330 in the morning, when you are cold, fed up and everyone else onboard is turned-in and snoring for Britain. Just take one boat at a time, starting with the closest. They are not moving very fast, so take your time and check that you are getting a positive bearing movement on everything that looks close. The best way to do this is to ensure that their lights are moving against the relatively static lights of distant fishing boats.

Unlike other fishing vessels, a trawler may show a masthead steaming light, and must if do so it is longer than 50 metres.

There are some pretty arcane rules for trawlers in close proximity to each other that are set out in Annex II to the rules. Frankly, these are not common and I have not included a mnemonic: they are designed to inform other fishing vessels rather than punters in pleasure boats. However, for the sake of completeness, here are the additional lights:

- *When shooting nets*
  2 white lights in a vertical line
- *When hauling in their nets*
  White over a red light
- *When nets caught on an obstruction*
  2 red lights in a vertical line

Vessels pair trawling (ie each is pulling one end of the net – not common) at night may have a searchlight directed forward and in the direction of the other vessel.

Vessels engaged in purse seining (this is where a fishing vessel deploys its nets in a circle, joins both ends and closes the bottom to form a 'purse') may show two vertically displaced yellow lights, flashing alternately.

Pilot vessels

Shapes	None.
Identification lights	White all-round light over a red all-round light.
Side and stern lights	Side and stern lights, only when under way.
Masthead steaming lights	None.
Anchor lights	Anchor lights appropriate to the length of vessel are shown together with pilot identification lights when at anchor and on pilotage duty.

Although no shapes are prescribed in the rules for a pilot boat, you will seldom see one which does not have the letters '**P I L O T**', or the local equivalent, painted down the side. Nothing too subtle here! They are also often seen flying a distinguishing flag vertically divided in half: red and white. This is the International Code, Flag H. Occasionally, the flag is divided horizontally rather than vertically: it is also used as a pilot signal.

Pilot boats are great enthusiasts. They are either going flat-out, or else they are stopped, recovering. Frequently they will loiter outside the approaches to ports at the Pilot Station, marked on Admiralty Charts with the symbol:

Provided that they are on pilotage duty, these vessels continue to show their identification lights at night[4] , even when stopped, or at anchor.

Don't confuse these lights with those of a fishing vessel. In practice, by day or night, there is no mistaking a pilot vessel and a fishing boat, even if you do muddle up the lights.

A pilot vessel's lights represent the pilot's weather-beaten red nose underneath his white seaman's cap.

Stern	Port side	Bow

By day

[4] If you were familiar with the previous edition of the rules you may remember pilot vessels being obliged to show a flare-up light at intervals of not more than 10 minutes, or an intermittent all-round white light. These have now been removed, although there is nothing to stop a pilot vessel from showing the intermittent white light to attract attention (Rule 36).

Towing vessels

Shapes	If the tow is greater than 200 m in length: a diamond shape, where best seen.
Identification lights	If the tow is less than 200 m in length: a second steaming light, vertically below the ship's masthead steaming light. If the tow is longer than 200 m: a third steaming light, below the other two.
Side and stern lights	Standard side and stern lights. A yellow towing light, vertically above the stern light, coloured yellow but with the same arcs as the stern light.
Masthead steaming lights	Masthead steaming lights, as for a power driven vessel.

If the towing vessel is longer than 50 m: a separate masthead light, above and abaft the others, as for a normal power driven vessel.

Stern	Side	Bow

Tug's lights when tow is less than 200 m.
(Tug less than 50 m in length.)

Tug's lights when tow is more than 200 m.
(Tug less than 50 m in length.)

The tow is measured from the stern of the tug to the stern of the tow.

This is one of the more complex sets of lights and shapes BUT you do see them surprisingly often. The good news is that tows are only considered to have manoeuvring limitations when they are showing Restricted in Ability to Manoeuvre shapes or lights in addition to the towing signals. If RAM lights and shapes are not shown, the tow can be expected to manoeuvre as a simple power driven vessel.

The towing signals are there to tell you what is happening and give an indication of the overall length of the tow. In effect, the towing vessel is lit like a power driven vessel, with the an extra stern light, coloured yellow, and one or two additional forward masthead steaming lights, depending on the length of the tow.

One can only feel a little sorry for tugboat crews: they don't move very fast and they spend most of their life being overtaken. None of the distinctive

masthead towing signals show in the 'overtaking sector', however. The yellow towing light is therefore designed as a cautionary light, shining aft to alert overtaking traffic.

The length of the tow is measured from the stern of the towing vessel to the stern of the last vessel in the tow.

If you have to tow someone, and are not fitted with additional towing lights, you have to do your best with what you have got to show that there is a towline between the two vessels involved. In particular, you will need to be able to illuminate the line at night if someone gets close to you and tries to cut in between.

I remember the shapes and lights like this: By day, if the tow is greater than 200 metres in length, it must be valuable. Therefore, both tug and tow show a diamond in the rigging.

By night, all the 'muscle' appears to be at the front with the extra forward steaming light(s). The yellow stern light is a cautionary warning to overtaking traffic.

Vessels being towed

Shapes	If the length of the tow exceeds 200 m, a diamond shape where best seen, just like the towing vessel. An inconspicuous or partly-submerged object being towed shows a diamond shape at the back end of the final vessel in the tow. An inconspicuous or partly-submerged object being towed that is longer than 200 m shows a second diamond shape at the front end.	

If wider than 25 m, they also carry all-round white lights on each beam. Finally, if longer than 100 m, they have intermediate all-round lights at intervals not exceeding 100 m. Dracones do not need to be lit at their front end.

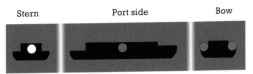

Stern   Port side   Bow

Vessels being towed.

Side and stern lights   Sidelights and a stern light (not shown on inconspicuous or semi-submerged objects being towed).

Steaming lights   None.

By day: Diamonds but only if tow exceeds 200 m.

Identification lights   None for a routine tow. However, inconspicuous or partly-submerged objects being towed have an all-round white light front and back.

Vessels being towed have to be lit to ensure that other people know that they are there. However, they aren't using their own power: therefore they don't need steaming lights.

▶

You really don't see inconspicuous or partly submerged objects being towed very often in NW Europe. However, there is a quaint logic about the distinguishing shapes and lights: by night, they carry white all-round lights fore and aft to get them noticed. If they are wide, white light on the port and starboard extremeties mark the width. The diamond shape just shows that there is something valuable there. More lights and diamonds if it is particularly long.

[5] If you have the inclination, take a look at the pictures of dracones in the Universal Rope website: www.universalrope.com/dracone.html ... then try to work out how you would spot one, let alone avoid it, at sea.

In 30-odd years at sea, I have never seen a dracone. In fact, it was only when compiling this book that I took the trouble to find out what this beast is[5]. For what it's worth, it is a great big rubber tube, which can be up to 300 feet in length, that is towed behind a tug to transport oil products lighter than sea water. They are coloured black, almost entirely awash and a complete pain in the neck to see. The moral is: if you can see a vessel with towing shapes or lights, and you can't see any vessel that is obviously being towed, proceed with great caution.

Vessels being pushed or towed alongside

Shapes	None.
Identification lights	None.
Side and stern lights	Sidelights in all cases. Stern light for a vessel being towed alongside. No sternlight for a vessel being pushed ahead.
Masthead lights	None.
Composite Unit	When the pushing vessel and the vessel being pushed are so rigidly connected that they can in all respects be considered a 'composite unit' – i.e. a single manoeuvring entity – they should be lit as a power-driven vessel.

*From the point of view of **the vessel doing the towing alongside or pushing**, the lights are precisely the same as a tug towing when the length of the tow is less than 200 metres. However, because in this case all the vessels are attached to each other, and there is no chance that anyone will cut between them, there is no need for a yellow towing light.*

Vessels being towed alongside or pushed both show sidelights at night. If a vessel being pushed showed a sternlight, however, it would blind the bridge of the pushing vessel. Therefore none is shown on vessels being pushed, although vessels being towed alongside, where the stern is abaft the tug's bridge, should show a stern light.

No shape is shown by any vessel in this case.

Towing alongside and pushing are quite common, and worth reading up. Vessels are normally pushed or towed alongside in sheltered harbours, and on rivers and inland waterways. At sea, conditions are often too rough to make anything other than an astern tow a sensible option. It is not always easy to manoeuvre an alongside tow in a cramped and busy harbour. Although they are technically power driven vessels under the rules, give them a break and keep out of their way if you can.

You will no doubt ask what a vessel 'rigidly connected in a composite unit' is (Rule 24b). This is when the tug and the vessel being pushed are designed to fit together hand-in-glove. They are not an issue: when joined up they are to all intents and purposes a power driven vessel.

Stern   Starboard side   Bow

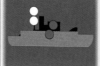

Towing alongside.

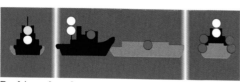

Pushing ahead.

More constrained vessels

That is the end of the vessels which are relatively capable of manoeuvring. We will now move onto the three categories of vessel that are telling you that they will have difficulty in obeying the manoeuvring rules.

Ships will display **Not Under Command (NUC)** shapes and lights when something has gone wrong that has a direct bearing on their manoeuvrability – power failure, steering gear broken, etc.

A more premeditated category, but one that still needs to be viewed with respect, is **Restricted in Ability to Manoeuvre (RAM)** where the limitations are imposed by the employment of the ship at that time. Cable laying is a good example, when the ship itself is perfectly serviceable, but the fact that she is connected to 2000 nautical miles of trans-Atlantic cable must to some extent limit her ability to get out of the way of a small boat.

Finally, an important category for yachtsmen to hoist in are **vessels Constrained by their Draught (CBD)**.

Not Under Command (NUC)

Shapes	2 balls in a vertical line where they can best be seen.
Identification lights	2 all-round red lights, one above the other.
Side and stern lights	Sidelights and stern light when making way (ie when moving through the water).
Masthead steaming lights	None.

Stern   Port side   Bow

Two clearly visible all round red lights.
If making way, show navigation lights and stern lights as well as NUC lights: if not making way, just NUC light.

By day:
two balls.

When Not Under Command lights and shapes are displayed, a vessel is generally suffering from a fairly major disability: through some exceptional circumstance [eg failure of steering gear] it is unable to manoeuvre as required by the rules. This is not an emergency signal, but you can bet your bottom dollar that there will be quite a lot of excitement on the bridge. The vessel may manoeuvre unpredictably: it certainly is not in a position to duck and weave to avoid traffic.

The rules regard NUC and RAM as the most severe manoeuvring disabilities for vessels under way: everyone should give way to vessels Not Under Command or Restricted in Ability to Manoeuvre.

Sidelights and stern lights are shown only when making way. Other ships need to know what direction she is heading in if she is moving so that they can take action to remain clear. If she is stationary, you just have to keep clear. There is no need to show steaming lights: the red lights at the masthead tell their own story.

I don't know how to put this nicely, but I always remember the lights and shapes of a vessel NUC on the grounds that the engineer has made a balls-up.
Therefore, 2 black balls and 2 red lights.

Restricted in Ability to Manoeuvre

Shapes — 3 shapes in a vertical line: a ball over a diamond, over a ball. A rigid replica of flag 'A' when engaged in diving operations and the vessel is too small to display the shapes fully.

Identification lights — 3 all-round lights where best seen: red over white over red.

Side and stern lights — Side and stern lights when making way through the water.

Masthead lights — Standard masthead lights, but only when making way through the water. When at anchor, but engaged on one of the activities that constitute RAM (Rule 3g), standard anchor lights plus RAM identification lights.

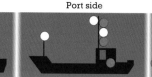

Stern   Port side   Bow

Three all-round vertical lights: red/white/red, plus sidelights, masthead lights and stern light if making way.

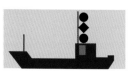

By day:
three vertical shapes:
ball/diamond/ball

A vessel is restricted in its ability to manoeuvre when it is unable – by virtue of her employment – to manoeuvre in accordance with the rules. As such, the limitations are quite similar to NUC, but self-imposed. Yachtsmen should note that sometimes (for instance when ships are launching or recovering aircraft) these vessels might be moving quite fast. Their limitations are often every bit as severe, however, as vessels Not Under Command.

Both RAM and NUC vessels show sidelights and stern lights only when making way (ie when moving through the water). Unlike vessels that are NUC, however, a vessel that is RAM must also show a masthead steaming light when making way.

Vessels less than 12 metres in length need only

display RAM shapes and lights if conducting diving operations.

The lights and shapes are very similar to those for a vessel not under command, but because it is deliberate, a small ray of sunshine has crept between the 2 balls or red lights – a diamond by day and a white light by night. A friend of mine from Liverpool once memorably described the lights as 'an Irish jam-buttie'[6].

Rule 3g defines 6 categories of employment that constitute Restricted in Ability to Manoeuvre. These are:

- A vessel engaged in laying, servicing or picking up a **N**avigation mark, submarine cable or pipeline.
- A vessel engaged in dredging, surveying or **U**nderwater operations.
- A vessel engaged in **R**eplenishment or transferring persons, provisions or cargo while underway.
- A vessel engaged in launching or recovery of **A**ircraft.
- A vessel engaged in **M**ineclearance operations.
- A vessel engaged in **T**owing operations that seriously restricts the towing vessel and tow in their ability to deviate from their course.

I have a pretty dull mnemonic for this: 'Never Use RAM Thoughtlessly'.

The best mnemonics are a little racy: I'm sure that you could dream up a more exotic one during a quiet night watch.

Three of these have their own peculiarities as far as lighting is concerned (they would, wouldn't they).

Towing has already been dealt with: the issue about RAM is that a tow is considered a normal manoeuvring unit unless it is specifically constrained, in which case, along with the towing lights and shapes, it also displays the lights or shapes appropriate to RAM.

The other two unusual categories are **dredgers** and **mine countermeasures vessels**. Since you are likely to see both (recognising that there are fewer mine countermeasures vessels in the USA than in Europe), I have dealt with these two as separate items below.

[6] In Liverpool, 'jam-buttie' is the name given to a jam sandwich.

Dredgers or vessels engaged in underwater operations

Shapes	3 shapes in a vertical line: a ball over a diamond, over a ball. Where an obstruction exists on one side or another: 2 balls in a vertical line on the side that the obstruction exists, 2 diamonds in a vertical line on the side that other vessels may pass.
Identification lights	3 all-round lights where best seen: red over white over red. Where an obstruction exists on one side or another: 2 all-round red lights in a vertical line on the side that the obstruction exists. 2 all-round green lights in a vertical line on the side that other vessels may pass.
Side and stern lights	Side and stern lights when making way through the water.
Masthead lights	Standard masthead lights, but only when making way through the water.

Stern   Starboard side   Bow

Dredger, or vessel engaged in underwater operations, foul on her port side.

Dredger, or vessel engaged in underwater operations, foul on her port side.

'Underwater operations' can consist of diving, using Remotely Operated Vehicles (little robotic diving machines for unmanned work under water), surveying or just about any sub-surface business that makes manoeuvring difficult. To qualify for RAM, the operations must cause severe manoeuvring restrictions.

The lights can seem confusing, particularly if you put together steaming lights, RAM lights, red & green obstruction lights and side lights. In practice, identification is generally more difficult on paper than afloat. However, you will be able to identify a dredger by day or by night because of its appearance – they are universally ugly ships[7] that are quite often floodlit at night, and there is usually a continuous metallic clanking from their dredging gear when they are working. You see a fair number of these around, and they are worth being able to recognise. In any case, if I was a yachtmaster examiner, I would consider this to be a great question to throw in.

When at anchor, but still dredging or engaged in underwater operations, standard anchor lights/shapes plus RAM lights/shapes are displayed.

A vessel engaged in diving operations that is too small to carry these lights and shapes need only carry: a rigid version of Flag 'A' by day and 3 all-round lights: red-white-red, mounted vertically, by night

**These are quite easy to remember.
RAM shapes/lights, and side, steaming and stern lights when making way (just like other RAM vessels).
The obstruction lights are like traffic lights: go on green and stop on red.
By day, you can pass the diamonds (diamonds are for ever) and will end up in trouble if you pass on the side with the balls (the 'balls-up' again, I'm afraid).**

[7] Somewhere in the world, there is probably a beautiful dredger. If so, I would like to take this opportunity to apologise unreservedly for my remarks to the designer, skipper and crew of this remarkable vessel.

Mine countermeasures vessels

Shapes	3 balls: one at the masthead, and one at each yard-arm of the forward mast. No 'RAM' shapes are displayed
Identification lights	3 all-round green lights: one at the masthead and one at each yard-arm of the forward mast. No 'RAM' lights are displayed.
Side and stern lights	Standard for power driven vessel.
Masthead lights	Standard for power driven vessel.

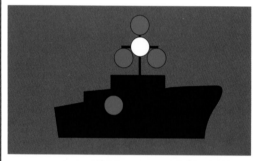

Mine clearance vessels exhibit three all round green lights or balls, plus lights for power vessel or lights/shapes for anchored vessel. Do not approach this vessel within 1000 m.

Mine Countermeasures is a relatively recent term which combines mine sweeping and mine hunting.

Mine sweeping is when long wires are deployed to cut a mine's mooring wire. This is a relatively indiscriminate activity, designed to sweep a clear path through a minefield.

Mine hunting is the activity of locating an individual mine, either on the bottom or moored, with a sonar device and then neutralising it with an explosive charge.

Although these vessels don't carry RAM shapes and lights, they are in every way Restricted in their Ability to Manoeuvre, and you are advised by the rules not to approach within 1000 metres (about ¹/₂ mile) of the vessel. The reason is that these vessels deal in high explosives: their job is inherently dangerous. Besides which, they could be deploying divers anywhere in their vicinity.

Even today, there are still a substantial number of live mines that have been dropped in the past and never been neutralised. Some are from recent conflicts, and many are old and corroded. These vessels still have a lot of 'real' work to do, and their business involves highly explosive and often very unstable underwater devices.

> ***'Three balls or three greens
> make minehunting machines'***

I remember a colleague standing beside me in the dusk on the flight deck of a frigate as a minehunter swept by during an exercise. 'I swear that those guys think they are driving around some kind of Christmas tree,' he said. 'Look at them: a green triangle by night, and they even have baubles to hang there by day.'

For some reason, it has always stuck in my mind.

Vessels constrained by their draught

Shapes	A cylinder, where best seen.
Identification lights	3 all-round red lights, one above the other.
Side and stern lights	As for a power driven vessel.
Masthead lights	As for a power driven vessel.

Stern	Starboard side	Bow

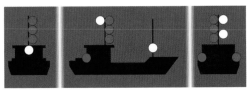

A vessel constrained by draught (eg a vessel confined to a limited channel) shows three vertical all round red lights as well as normal navigation lights.

By day:
a vertical cylinder

Technically, these vessels are not 'Restricted in their Ability to Manoeuvre' because they are simply power driven vessels that don't have the geographical freedom to manoeuvre.

There is an old joke: 'What do you call a 20 stone bouncer who is about to hit you?' The

answer, of course, is anything he wants. It's a bit like that with a vessel constrained by its draught. It's heavy, it's committed to the channel and it can't easily stop. When it wants you to get out of its way ... you do.

Big ships will nearly always declare themselves to be constrained by their draught in close pilotage waters. Sometimes, the lights and shapes may be altered by local by-laws: always read a pilot book before entering a strange port. You will frequently see vessels constrained by their draught in the approaches to major ports: when you do, keep well out of the way. Only vessels Not Under Command and Restricted in their Ability to Manoeuvre are absolved from the necessity to keep out of the way of a vessel constrained by its draught (Rule 18d).

Three red lights: these vessels have even less freedom of manoeuvre than NUC. (This may or may not be true, but it is how I remember it!)

In the RN we sometimes play a flight deck game called 'the rat in a drainpipe'. Someone makes a heavy rat-shaped creature out of masking tape and drops it down about a 2-metre length of opaque pipework, which terminates about 30 cm from the deck. The point of the game is that you stand by the pipe, armed with a broomstick. You see the 'rat' being dropped into the top of the pipe and, using your exquisite sense of timing, you try to swipe it as it emerges from the bottom. Anyway, vessels constrained by their draught have about the same ability to manoeuvre as that rat.
That is my explanation of why they show a bit of the drainpipe (a black cylinder) by day.

Vessels that cannot manoeuvre

All the vessels up to now have been under way – ie not attached to the shore or the sea bed in any way. We will now have a look at two sorts of vessel that simply cannot manoeuvre to keep clear of you: **vessels at anchor** and **vessels aground**. Straight away you will realise that the masthead steaming lights, side and stern lights, which are only shown by vessels that are under way, are redundant. The lights (and the sound signals come to that) have to be recognisably different from those of a vessel under way in order to make it easy for mariners to realise that the onus of collision avoidance is on them[8].
Although the rules are not specific about this, a vessel that is securely moored to a buoy

may consider itself to be at anchor, but a vessel with the anchor dragging should not. It is good practice in a yacht to use your anchor light when moored to a buoy, particularly if you are close to a busy waterway, or if you have rowed ashore on a dark night, so that it can act as your beacon on the way home. Many is the time (and we are not alone here) when Susie and I have rowed round the pitch-black moorings of British or French ports looking for the boat, desperately wishing that we had remembered the anchor light when we went ashore in mid-afternoon.

[8] This is not always as easy as it seems. Be careful of moored objects (including anchored ships) in a strong tidal stream.

Vessels at anchor

Shapes   A ball in the forepart of the ship, where best seen.
If less than 7 metres in length, when anchored clear of narrow channels, fairways or anchorages, or normal navigation routes, need not exhibit the ball.

Identification lights   A white all-round light in the forepart of the ship, where best seen. A second white all-round light in the stern of the vessel, but lower than that at the forward end.Vessels of less than 50 m in length need show only one white all-round light, where it can best be seen. Any vessel at anchor may show additional lights to illuminate her decks. A vessel of 100 m or more in length must do this.

Note: Yachts over 7 m must display an anchor light. Under 7 m need not, unless near a fairway or anchorage.

By day:
one ball.

You might be thinking that if you see two white lights, one higher than the other, it could be the steaming lights of a vessel under way. But in that case, where are the sidelights? And the big give-away is the deck working lights that are mandatory in big ships, and optional in smaller ones.

The distinction between fore and aft is important. It is distinguished by the fact that the forward anchor light is higher than that on the stern (this is of course the opposite way round to steaming lights, where the after light is higher). This allows you to determine which end the cable is streamed from and so, hopefully, avoid the risk of fouling it.

On a big ship you will sometimes have to look quite hard to see the anchor ball, which large merchant ships often display from a small stub mast right over the bows. Sometimes, the first indication that you will have that a ship is at anchor will be a sight of the cable falling into the water under the bows. Returning from France to Portsmouth last year, we sailed east of the Isle of Wight and came across a big ship in Sandown Bay. It appeared to be a con-verging course. It was only after a few manoeuvres (a little embarrassing in hindsight) that I saw the ball hanging from the foremast, and a cable deployed from the bow. Susie, my wife, took a long time to let me live down the fact that I had taken so much trouble to avoid a totally immobile ship.

Under 50 m	**Over 50 m** (obligatory) **Under 50 m** (optional)
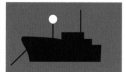	
All round white light forward. Larger vessels will usually also show deck working lights.	A second white light aft (lower than for'd light).

Vessels aground

Shapes   Three balls in a vertical line. Not necessary for a vessel aground that is less than 12 metres in length.

Identification lights   Anchor lights (as above), but without the need to illuminate the deck if longer than 100 m. Two all-round red lights in a vertical line. Not necessary either for a vessel aground that is less than 12 metres in length.

There is no need for the deck working lights because the two red lights distinguish this from a ship at anchor. Also, it cannot be confused with a vessel Not Under Command, which does not show steaming lights.

Stern	Port side	Bow

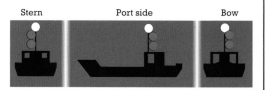

Under 50 m:
two all round red lights plus anchor light.

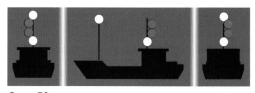

Over 50 m:
two all round red lights plus anchor lights.

▶

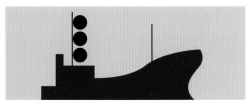

Three vertical balls.

Note: vessel under 12 m need not exhibit lights or shapes when aground

There is a bit of a trap here. If you think about it, there is a sort of progression and logic about shapes and lights:

- *At anchor – one ball – one white light*
- *Not under command – 2 balls – 2 red lights*

***Do not be duped** into connecting 3 balls (aground) with 3 red lights (vessel constrained by its draught)*

I always remembered the 3 balls and the anchor lights with 2 red all-round lights as: 'a total balls-up'. Less irreverently, it could be 'not under command and at anchor'. It makes a sort of quirky sense when you sit down and think about it.

Some oddballs

Hovercraft

Shapes	None: the shape of a hovercraft is unmistakable, it makes a lot of noise, and it is usually shrouded in spray.
Identification lights	All-round yellow flashing light at 120 flashes per minute or more.
Side and stern lights	As for a power driven vessel.
Masthead lights	As for a power driven vessel.

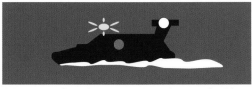

A **hovercraft** underway at night shows a flashing yellow light plus normal navigation lights.

There are not a lot of commercial hovercraft companies still operating. One prominent route is in the eastern Solent, where a regular service is conducted between Portsmouth and the Isle of Wight. These vessels are really not manoeuvrable: they skid massively during a turn and, while they are bound to operate as power driven vessels by the rules, you would do them a kindness to give them a very significant berth when you can.

Also, bear in mind that they are very susceptible to the wind and can be making good a course that is up to 45° away from their heading; at night,

therefore, their navigation lights may be misleading, particularly if there is a strong cross-wind.

Don't confuse with submarines, which are quieter, slower and are found in a very different habitat. Submarines, however, often use a yellow flashing light when operating on the surface. UK submarines use a continuous flashing amber light, whilst US Navy submarines carry an amber light that flashes a group of 3 every 6 seconds.

'If it has 3 yellow flashes, it surfaces with splashes[9]'.

Seaplanes

Shapes	None: the shape of a seaplane is unmistakable.
Identification lights	None.
Side and stern lights	As for a power driven vessel (or as close to that as possible).
Masthead lights	As for a power driven vessel (or as close to that as possible).

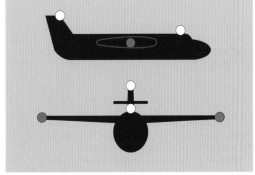

One or two steaming lights. May also have a red obstruction light.

[9] My thanks to the Director of Auxiliary, 7th US Coast Guard District. www.dirauxannex.org/ruleof.html.

Clearly, it may not be possible to get all the lights right because of the shape of a seaplane: they are nevertheless required to get as close to the proper light lay-out as they can. They often have sidelights in the wingtips and a stern light in the tail. They may show a 'mast-head light' forward.

Seaplanes are required to keep clear of all other vessels and avoid impeding their navigation (Rule 18e). If push comes to shove, however, they should be considered as normal power driven vessels.

Seaplanes are very much more common in the USA and Canada than they are in Europe. There are often special operating areas delineated on the chart for seaplanes, where boats are advised to keep clear.

Vessels propelled by oars

Shapes	None. Except perhaps two long bits of wood sticking out from the side of the boat.
Identification lights	A vessel propelled by oars may show the lights of a sailing vessel (see page 17).
Side and stern lights	If not, a white torch should be available to avert a collision.

White torch ready if needed.

A large fighting galley, packed with slaves operating the oars, might these days show more than a white torch. In that case, they will be the lights appropriate for a sailing vessel of that size.

You and I are most likely to be interested in this rule as it applies to our boats' tenders. If you are out in a small black rubber boat in the middle of the night, on your way back from a few drinks in a waterside bar, responsibility for keeping safe is very much yours. Remember to pack a reliable, strong and waterproof white torch, and remember to check that it works. It is all too easy to be run over for want of this simple precaution.

Police boats

Police boats are reasonably common, particularly in busy and congested waters. They are lit as power driven vessels with – you guessed it – a flashing blue all-round light when they need to show who they are. By day, these boats tend to carry the letters '**P O L I C E**' unmistakably painted on the side.

Lifeboats

British lifeboats also carry a blue flashing light that they use when operational. It is carried along with standard navigation lights.

Warships

All warships are painted a drab grey or off-grey colour and even at a very great distance there is something about their centrally-stacked superstructure that makes them stand out from merchant ships at long range. Don't always expect them to behave like normal ships: unlike a merchant vessel, which tends to plough on in a straight line and at a constant speed, warships will often manoeuvre violently and without warning, thus thoroughly upsetting the chefs trying to prepare lunch below.

Their lights moreover will sometimes be unusual. Submarines on the surface might have one or more of their lights very close to the water, and frequently obscured. Long warships may show just one navigation light. You will often see warships with a set of red all-round obstruction lights at the mast-head to prevent helicopters from flying into the mast, and you will occasionally see a ship with a helicopter on the flight deck which has a set of lights all of its own. These can be confusing. Finally, an aircraft carrier's lights might be displaced off the centre line, and it may even have more than one set of side lights. The trick, when you see a warship, is to remain flexible and give it as wide a berth as you can.

Liners

I was once on a dived operation in a submarine, feeling extraordinarily tired, unwashed and under a great deal of pressure when, at sunset, we were passed by a large cruise liner. Watching it through the periscope, you could see people wandering casually along the decks: you could work out where the swimming pools were, a delicious meal was no doubt being prepared and people were just having a quick bath before popping down to the bar for a pre-dinner drink. You could almost hear the music and laughter!

The thing that I remember about it was the way in which it was lit. Of course it had side lights, masthead steaming lights and a stern light, but they were almost invisible against the universal lighting of the upper decks and the cabins. There were lights everywhere. The point is that you will almost certainly recognise it as a liner, but you may have a bit of trouble working out its orientation.

Oil Rigs

Oil rigs tend to operate in herds. You occasionally come across an isolated one, that has probably wandered off from its friends, but more generally you will find lots of them peacefully grazing away together in the oil and gas fields. Permanent rigs are reasonably well charted, so you would think that a moderately alert mariner with an up-to-date chart would know what to expect. If only life was that simple!

The problem comes with the rigs that have adopted the more solitary lifestyle. Many companies send out exploratory rigs which spend only a short time in any particular spot before moving on. They are almost never shown on the chart, although their position is well documented in Notices to Mariners.

Oil rigs tend to be well lit. Many have a plume of flame burning off the unwanted gasses into the atmosphere. And you are likely to see a few small safety boats loitering in the water nearby. The good news is that they are stationary. Give them a wide berth – at least half a mile if you can, and don't forget to check on the chart in case there are any navigation warnings or restricted areas around the rigs.

Signals to attract attention

Rule 36

If necessary to attract the attention of another vessel, any vessel may make light or sound signals that cannot be mistaken for any signal authorised elsewhere in these Rules, or may direct the beam of her searchlight in the direction of the danger, in such a way as not to embarrass any vessel. Any light to attract the attention of another vessel shall be such that it cannot be mistaken for any aid to navigation. For the purpose of this Rule the use of high intensity intermittent or revolving lights, such as strobe lights, shall be avoided.

This message about how to attract attention is unambiguous: do it in a way that can't be mistaken for anything else, and don't embarrass other vessels by your actions.

You may well want to let someone know that you are there, particularly if you are crossing a busy shipping lane in a small, inconspicuous boat. If the other vessel has not taken avoiding action, and shows no sign of recognising your existence on the planet, you start to feel very small indeed. And stressed. You might try some of the following:

• Turn away to reduce the closing rate.
• If you can do so, call him up on Channel 16 VHF, preferably by name.
• By night, illuminate your sails or flash a searchlight across his bearing, trying to avoid blinding the officer of the watch. Don't train a light directly on his bridge and leave it there. If the officer of the watch was keeping a poor look-out before, it will certainly not be improved by robbing him of his night vision.
• Make sound signals if it will help (5 or more short blasts might be appropriate).

Do not:
• Use a high-intensity strobe. Although where you might find one in a boat in the middle of the ocean is a mystery to me: 'I'll bring you up a cup of coffee, darling, just as soon as I can find a mug under this pile of high-intensity strobes.'
• Use distress flares. They carry one meaning and one meaning only: that you need to be helped or rescued.

Common flag hoists

There are many more than this; these are the most common.

	Flag Hoist	What it looks like	Notes
Diving operations in progress	**ALFA**		Small boats often show a rigid replica of the flag.
Man overboard	**OSCAR**		Carried on a lot of man overboard danbuoys, or ships that are engaged in picking up a man overboard (and therefore likely to be manoeuvring violently).
Proceed past me slowly	**ROMEO YANKEE**		You may or may not see 'ROMEO YANKEE' flown below a long red and white pennant. Ignore the pennant: it is the 'Answer Pennant', merely naval signal short-hand for *'Read this hoist in accordance with the International Code of Signals, and not as a military code.'*
You are standing into danger	**UNIFORM**		This is sometimes still used to draw a vessel's attention to the fact that it needs to change course. Sometimes accompanied by the morse equivalent: • • —
Distress	**NOVEMBER CHARLIE**		This is one of the proscribed distress signals that you MUST know (see Section 7). An alternative is to fly any square flag with a ball above or below it.

3 How to recognise the other vessel: sound signals

Sound signals don't only happen in fog. **Fog signals** are used in restricted visibility to alert other vessels in the vicinity to your presence. There is a completely distinct set of sound signals, called **manoeuvring signals**, that are used by ships in sight of each other to help them understand each other's actions. The two sets are therefore almost mutually exclusive.

A few quick definitions:

Prolonged blast: A blast of 4 – 6 seconds' duration.

Short blast: A blast of about 1 second's duration.

Signalling devices to be carried by vessels: A vessel of more than 100 m in length should carry a whistle, bell and gong, or something that sounds like one.
A vessel greater than 12 m in length, but less than 100 m, should carry a whistle and a bell. A vessel of less than 12 m in length can carry a whistle and bell. If not, it should have an efficient sound-signalling device onboard.

You should always carry a whistle of some sort in your boat - and make it as loud as possible. If you use an aerosol-powered horn, make sure that you carry a few spare aerosols onboard.

Sound signals on navigation marks

Explosive: Detonation of an explosive device. Sounds like a gun. I have never heard one.
Diaphone (Dia): This device, powered by compressed air, creates a low droning hooting noise, actually on two frequencies simultaneously. It sounds deeply depressing and sometimes ends in a 'grunt'! If you have never heard one, try the 'World's only diaphone website':

http://diaphone.tripod.com/diaphone_sounds.htm
Foghorn (horn): Uses compressed air or electricity to operate a diaphragm
Reed: Operated by compressed air. Pitch varies, but is generally higher than a diaphone or horn.

On buoys, you are likely to hear:
Bells: These may be either mechanical, or powered by compressed wave action,
Whistles: in which case, the sound will clearly be irregular. Much shorter range than
Gongs: sound signals on shore-based lights or beacons.

These will all be marked on the chart, and they will be designed to ensure that they are positively different from any sound signal that a vessel might make.

Manoeuvring signals for vessels in sight of each other

Manoeuvring signals are extremely common in congested waterways, and you do need to know them by heart, if possible. They are made by vessels in sight of each other to clarify what actions each is taking. According to the rules, they are mandatory when in sight of other vessels and making a course alteration to reduce the risk of collision[1]. In practice, they tend to occur only when there is some ambiguity or urgency over the alteration of course.

If you look closely at Rule 34(a), you will see that manoeuvring signals are to be made only

[1]The actual wording of Rule 34(a) is: *'When vessels are in sight of each other, a power driven vessel underway, when manoeuvring as authorised or required by these rules, shall indicate that manoeuvre by the following signals on her whistle:'*

by power-driven vessels. All other signals, including the supplementary manoeuvring signals made by flashing light, can be made by any vessel. Tuck this away in your brain, but don't pay too much attention to it. I have never heard a sailing boat making manoeuvring signals, despite being in some fairly congested sailing waters, but if you do for some reason need to make a manoeuvring signal under sail, my guess is that the people around you will understand what you are trying to tell them and react accordingly.

Some manoeuvring sound signals may be supplemented by simultaneous flashes from a white all-round light at the vessel's masthead. This is very rare: I have only seen it once in almost 30 years at sea, when I was keeping an eye on a Polish trawler off Torbay. I remember that we were all deeply impressed by his knowledge of the rules.

Turning and slowing down signals

I am altering my course to starboard	One short blast	Only used when vessels are in sight of each other
I am altering my course to port	Two short blasts	May be supplemented by flashing a white all-round light from the masthead
I am operating astern propulsion	Three short blasts	

'Starboard' has an odd number of letters, and an odd number of whistle blasts
'Port' has an even number of letters and an even number of blasts

'Half as-tern', or even 'Full as-tern' both have 3 syllables and 3 blasts.
Bear in mind that this does not mean the vessel is necessarily moving astern – merely that he has started operating astern propulsion, and so may just be slowing down.

Vessels in sight of each other

One short blast
I am altering my course to starboard.

Two short blasts
I am altering my course to port.

Three short blasts
My engines are running astern.

Overtaking Signals in a narrow channel or fairway

I intend to overtake on your starboard side	Two prolonged blasts followed by one short blast	Only used when vessels are in sight of each other and in a narrow channel or fairway
I intend to overtake on your port side	Two prolonged blasts followed by two short blasts	These signals are not supplemented by flashing a white all-round light from the masthead
I am happy for you to overtake	One prolonged, one short, one prolonged, one short blast	

These signals are mandatory but, in my experience, they are relatively rare, partly because the number of places that you can overtake in a narrow channel are limited, but more convincingly because most people have pilots embarked in this sort of waterway, and pilots – sensibly – use VHF.

As a yachtsman, you are most likely to come across them when you are already highly stressed, dodging man-eating merchant ships on your way up a busy canal into Rotterdam. At times like this you will have your hands full without having to scamper off and look up the signals, so you might as well learn them in advance.

▶

If someone signals his intention to overtake you, and you don't like the idea, you should make the 'uncertainty signal' of 5 short blasts (below).

These are easy enough to remember.
The 2 long blasts represent the 2 ships in line astern, one impatiently waiting to overtake the other. The short blasts represent the side that the ship will overtake in accordance with the turning signals (above).

The 'OK, I'm ready for you' signal is a sort of bored man tapping his fingers on the top of the radar display 'dum-ti-dum-ti' while he is waiting for the overtaking vessel to get past and out of his way.

Vessels in a narrow channel in sight of each other

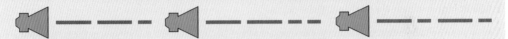

Two long & one short blasts	**Two long & two short blasts**	**Morse Code 'C'**
I intend to overtake you	I intend to overtake you	I agree to be
on your starboard side.	on your port side.	overtaken.

Uncertainty

| | | Only used when vessels are in sight of each other |
| **I don't understand your intentions** | At least 5 'short and rapid' blasts | May be supplemented by flashing a white all-round light from the masthead |

This is not restricted to narrow channels, and can be useful anywhere if vessels are in sight of each other. Living as I do on the waterfront of Portsmouth Harbour, I now realise that this signal is a totally predictable seasonal phenomenon. From about April to September the waters are full of sailing and motor boats. The poor ferry skippers and merchant ships have a blizzard of small white boats to negotiate every time they enter and leave port. As a result, five short blasts can frequently be heard around the harbour during the summer months. It's a bit like the first cuckoo of spring: hear the sound and start getting the garden furniture out.

Five (or more) blasts
Your intentions are not
understood. Keep clear.

Approaching a blind corner

Approaching a bend or other area of a fairway when vessels might be obscured	1 prolonged blast	In a narrow channel or fairway. This signal gives advance warning of your approach to vessels that are out of sight: there is no point in signalling with a flashing light as well

Vessels hearing this signal from behind a bend should reply in kind with a single prolonged blast.

This is not as simple as it seems. I used this signal once in a very tight cliff-lined channel in the depths of the Norwegian Fjords. Sure enough, almost immediately there was an answering signal from around the corner. I got as close to the starboard side of the channel as possible in what was a pretty hopeless effort to make enough space for the other ship that was about to appear from behind the granite. It was only after I had all-but scraped the paint off the ship's side that the pilot turned round and informed me that: 'There is often a very strong echo at this point of the fjord, and you should not think that another ship is coming – ja?' I have always been suspicious of the nordic sense of humour from that date to this.

You may wish to use this signal for yacht-to-yacht signalling when negotiating a narrow, sinuous river or canal, but a yacht's signalling apparatus is unlikely to be heard on the bridge of even the smallest merchant ship.

However, if you hear a large ship making this signal when you are in a yacht, take it as a good hint to clear the fairway to allow him to come by. It will by definition only be used when a big ship's reaction time is limited, so make it easy for them.

The purists will question whether a sound signal from around a blind corner can honestly be said to apply to vessels in sight of each other. It is, however, intended to be an extension of the clear visibility rules, and is not applied in restricted visibility.

One long blast
I am approaching a bend in the channel.

Sound signals in restricted visibility

In the following section, as a matter of shorthand, I have referred to sound signals in restricted visibility as **fog signals**. You should, however, be aware that there are numerous other causes of restricted visibility, all of which call for these sounds to be made. Some are set out in Rule 3 (l), and include: fog, mist, falling snow, heavy rainstorms, sandstorms, etc.

However caused, reduced visibility is the most dangerous situation encountered by the majority of yachtsmen. It changes everything: you have different manoeuvring rules (see page 52), your level of uncertainty rises, you have substantially less warning time to avoid other ships, and you have to concentrate very much more on collision avoidance. It is not very pleasant, and since yachting ought to be a pleasant experience, especially given the amount of money that we all invest in it, I would advise yachtsmen to avoid fog like the plague.

Inevitably, however, there will be times when one is caught out in a small boat in fog. It is on these occasions that you will need to have a good working knowledge of fog signals. You must make sure that you can identify the other vessels, and that you know both how they will react, and what you must do to remain safe.

You should perhaps realise that fog increases the tension levels markedly on the bridge of bigger ships too. Ships start relying more on radar, but not all radars are perfectly tuned, and small contacts will suddenly get lost in the ground clutter, just at the range where it is most important to keep an eye on them. Big ships post lookouts in the bow, but they sometimes lose concentration, and in some vessels there may even be a language problem when they report to the bridge. And from time to time even the most professional ships make mistakes.

There was one particularly painful moment when, as Captain of a frigate, I managed to embarrass myself thoroughly for exactly this reason.

We had planned to pick up an Admiral just outside Plymouth breakwater. He was expected at 0915 in the morning, and with a precision that the Royal Navy likes to pride itself on, we were are the appointed place, slowing down and ready to collect him, with less than a minute to go. It was all going like clockwork, except for one thing: visibility was about 200 metres. The officer of the watch and I were scanning the horizon, such as it was, looking for the Admiral's boat: we could see nothing, and no small craft had been reported on radar coming out from the Sound. I was beginning to think that he had changed his mind so I got on the VHF and called up his boat to ask where they were. Instead of the measured tones of the cox'n that I had been expecting, I got the Admiral himself:

'We're 25 yards off your quarter, you idiot, and have been waiting here for 5 minutes for you to welcome us onboard!'

Believe me, if an Admiral's launch can escape the notice of a warship's radar, with endless numbers of people on watch, it is very much easier for a yacht to slip under the guard of a merchant ship or ferry. This is particularly true in the middle of the night or the early hours of the morning, when people may well be less alert.

My moral is this:
In poor visibility, tread carefully.

There are a number of things that you really ought to be aware of:

1. **You really cannot rely on a yacht showing up on another vessel's radar screen.** A ship's radar is likely to be altogether more accurate and discriminating than the types that most of us carry in our yachts (although I would not always bet on it). But even if you buy a top-of-the-range radar reflector and get it properly orientated, you will still only show up as a small intermittent target. If it's rough, or if there are a lot of rocks, buoys or other boats around, you may well get lost in radar screen clutter. So, don't rely on superior technology or superior knowledge in the other guy to keep your boat safe.

2. **The rules change when vessels are not in sight of each other.** In restricted visibility you need to switch into a different decision-making process, guided by a different set of parameters (see page 52).

3. **Yacht radars are not good at bearings**. A radar's scanner defines the width of the beam. The wider the aerial, the narrower the beam, and the narrower the beam, the more accurate will be the bearing read-out. Most yachts are forced by geometry and by cost to compromise on scanner size, and as with so many things in life, size

matters. In fog, using your radar, you will sometimes find it difficult to get a good grasp on another vessel's bearing movement. Rule one of survival at sea applies here: if in doubt, assume that the other ship is about to collide with you, and act accordingly.

4. **Your foghorn is about as much use as a chocolate fireguard if you want to alert big ships to your presence.** Where it is worth it's weight in gold, however, is telling other yachts and fishing vessels where you are, so don't stop using it. Last summer Susie and I came across a stopped fishing boat just south of Jersey. If he had not been making intermittent signals on the foghorn we may have been looking the other way when he suddenly loomed out of the mist at 200 metres' range.

5. **Many merchant ships do not slow down appreciably when navigating through fog.** When crossing a busy shipping lane you can still expect some ships to be travelling at up to 25 knots. Even at 15 knots, if you assume that you can hear its foghorn at 3 miles, you will have something in the order of 12 minutes to ensure that you are safe if you are crossing his track. This is not long to work out what is going on, react, and then have time to get clear. Turning away to put him on the stern, however, reduces his closing rate to 9 knots and increases this warning time to 20 minutes. Always have your options running through your mind in poor visibility.

What can you do with your limited resources in fog?

1. Make yourself as visible as possible with a good radar reflector and navigation lights. Brief your crew to act as lookouts and to listen for other vessels' fog signals.
2. Slow down to a safe speed. Particularly if you are in a motor boat.
3. If you are sailing, start your engine (handy, but noisy), or have it immediately available.
4. If you carry radar, close up your most experienced crew on the radar for collision avoidance.
5. Put on your lifejackets and have the grab-bag handy. If you think this a little melodramatic, you are wrong. In any case, it is amazing how reassuring it is to your crew.
6. Have good intelligence: know where the traffic is likely to be coming from and going to. If possible, keep clear of the busiest lanes; if you can't, be ready to parallel the direction of traffic if things start getting stressful.
7. Finally, know your fog signals; this helps you make informed decisions – that is what this chapter is all about.

FOG SIGNALS

The most important thing in fog is to be able to identify what is out there. In practice, this is not very difficult: 99.5% of all fog signals that you will ever hear are those of a power-driven vessel under way. Power-driven vessels are dangerous enough for a small boat – anything else will, if anything, be more of a problem, so do what you can to keep out of their way.

Power driven vessels

Power driven vessel under way, making way	One prolonged blast	Intervals of not more than 2 minutes
Power driven vessel under way, but not making way	Two prolonged blasts	

This is the 'default' sound signal in restricted visibility.

You could go through an entire lifetime at sea and not hear anything but one prolonged blast every 2 minutes in fog.

Very occasionally, one hears 2 blasts, but not very often for the simple reason that most people now use radar, and have no need to stop when visibility reduces.

Vessels in restricted visibility

One long blast
every 2 minutes
Power vessel underway.

Two long blasts
every 2 minutes
Power vessel stopped.

The bad guys

If you thought ordinary power driven vessels are untrustworthy in fog, this is the true rogues' gallery. Most of these vessels will have more on their mind than the need to stay clear of other shipping, and the best thing that you can do to help is to stay well out of their way.

Vessel **N**ot under command		
Vessel **R**estricted in its ability to manoeuvre		
Vessel **C**onstrained by its draught	One prolonged blast followed by two short blasts	Intervals of not more than 2 minutes
Sailing vessel		
Vessel **E**ngaged in fishing	(− · ·)	
Vessel engaged in **T**owing or pushing another vessel		

If a vessel is making this signal, she does not make the power driven vessel signal.

As a small sailing yacht, I would normally start my engine when the fog comes down, so as to increase my freedom of manoeuvre; that done, I start making signals for a power driven vessel (above). Sailing boats that are sailing should use the signal prescribed here (− · ·)

▶

The interesting thing is that fog, in the eyes of the rule-makers, puts fishing boats and vessels Not Under Command on the same scale of vulnerability. This is because all of these vessels are in some way hampered, and the effect of fog is to exacerbate its position.

I use a mnemonic for these categories:
'No Radar Can See Every Target'.

The sound signal looks like a tug with 2 small vessels in tow
– and applies to all 6 categories of vessel.

One long & 2 short blasts
every 2 minutes. Vessels under sail. Also:
vessels fishing, towing, NUC, RAM, CBD.

… And one more

Vessel being towed, or the last vessel in a tow (if manned)	One prolonged blast followed by 3 short blasts (– • • •)	Signal should be made immediately after that of the towing vessel

This is like the towing signal (above), only the final vessel in the tow is pointing out that it is also there.

To avoid confusing other ships, it is made immediately after the towing vessel's signal.

If you want to preserve your no-claims bonus, try to make sure that the two signals, that of the tow and that of the towing vessel, are both drawing past you in the same direction.

Morse Code 'B'
every 2 minutes
Vessel under tow (if manned).

Vessels at anchor

If you think about it, a vessel at anchor in fog is about as dangerous as an uncharted rock suddenly appearing in the middle of previously navigable water. If you hear the bells and gongs, and you have a good idea where the source of the sound is, bear in mind that the ship will stretch a long way in one direction and the cable may well extend some distance in the other.

By the time that the ship is visible, the anchor and deck lights may be above your sight line, or even obscured behind the side of the ship.

These are dangerous beasts in fog, and that is why they are invited to make the sounds every minute rather than every two minutes.

Let's face it: your day would be totally spoiled if you piled into the side of an anchored tanker in fog. The irony is that the people onboard the tanker probably wouldn't even notice that you had done it. Happily, the sound signals are designed to be completely different from those made under way. They are also of very much shorter range, so if you do hear them, you can be certain that you are close.

▶

Vessel of less than 100 m in length at anchor	5 seconds ringing of a bell	
Vessel of more than 100 m in length at anchor	5 seconds ringing of a bell forward followed immediately by 5 seconds ringing of a gong aft	Not more than 1 minute
Vessel at anchor giving warning of his position and indicating the possibility of collision with an approaching vessel	As above (appropriate to the length of the anchored vessel) but in addition one short, one long and one short blast (· — ·)	

A ship under way would never rely on a ringing bell to keep other vessels clear; in fog and at anchor, however, it is a very distinctive noise and, if you hear it, you will recognise it.

The gong (or something that resembles one) is designed to let you know where this big slab of steel ends: the gong, being the symbol of a big movie company, is reserved for the place where the films are shown – in the accommodation which is generally aft.

Although the rules say that the gong should be sounded immediately after the bell, a big ship's bell often cannot be heard from the accommodation aft, and this part of the rule may well not be achievable.

> **The signal (· — ·) is a little pictogram of a big ship surrounded**
> **by a couple of little ones that he is uncertain about.**
> **For those of you who recognise the letter 'R' in morse (· — ·),**
> **the classic mnemonic for this is:**
> **'R you coming close to me?'**

Vessels at anchor

May sound morse Code 'R' (· — ·) to warn approaching vessel.

Rapid ringing of bell for 5 seconds every minute.

Vessel over 100 m at anchor

Bell rung forward. Then gong rung rapidly aft for 5 seconds.

Vessel of less than 12m in length at anchor	Is not obliged to give the above signals, but may instead make some efficient sound signal	Intervals of not more than 2 minutes

Vessels aground

Vessel aground	As for a vessel of that length at anchor, but with 3 distinct rings of the bell before and after the 5 seconds ringing	Not more than 1 minute
	The gong and whistle signals may be used as appropriate	

This signal is also registered by the ship's bell, and includes the 'at anchor' signal of 5 seconds ringing. At each end of it, however, the poor old vessel has to come clean with 3 distinct rings: 'I'm a-ground.' It's a sort of confessional.

Vessels aground

Three rings of bell	Anchor signal	Three rings of bell

Vessel of less than 12 m in length aground	Is not obliged to give the above signals, but may instead make some efficient sound signal	Intervals of not more than 2 minutes

Good news for yachtsmen: you can go aground in the fog and no one will ever notice: you will sound just like a regular floating yacht!

Pilot vessel, engaged in pilotage duties	The appropriate fog signal for a power driven vessel, depending on whether she is under way, or at anchor (we will draw a veil over the possibility of a pilot vessel running aground in fog)	As appropriate to the circumstances
	In addition, four short blasts	

The 4 short blasts actually signify the letter 'H' in morse, which is the same as the red and white flag, vertically divided, that these vessels fly by day.

You can remember this in any way that you wish:
There is no other vessel that will do one prolong blast (for a power driven vessel)
followed by 4 short ones (signifying a pilot vessel): even the last
vessel of the tow sounds only one prolonged blast and 3 short ones.

If you want, you can count the syllables and get it to say:
'I'M A PI-LOT'.
It just depends on how your brain is wired up.

4 Manoeuvring rules

The previous two chapters have dispatched the difficult stuff – how to recognise other vessels. All that remains to be done is to have a quick look at the application of the rules. You are out there at sea and you see another ship closing you on a steady bearing: who should give way to whom, and what is the safest way of doing it?

In fact, the more astute readers will have noticed that the rules don't actually refer to 'right of way'. They talk about a 'give-way vessel' (green in our diagrams)and a 'stand-on vessel' (red in our diagrams). The reason for this is that when push comes to shove and a collision appears imminent, *both* vessels are obliged to act. Therefore, even if the rules define you as the stand-on vessel in a particular situation, you cannot just switch off and go below for a cup of tea. You must always be satisfied that sufficient action is being taken by the other vessel to avoid a collision: if you aren't happy, you must do something.

Until that point is reached, it is immensely helpful if the stand-on vessel maintains its course and speed as required by the rules; there is nothing worse than trying to avoid a ship that is jigging around.

But let's just wind the range out a little more. Big merchant ships in open water are likely to take avoiding action at a range of 2 – 3 miles. So if the range is, say 5 miles or more, and you think that a risk of collision could develop, you may want to consider whether a small alteration of course or speed by yourself at that point would just make the problem go away. It's as simple as that: a bit like a soap powder advertisement. Take two ships, add a sprinkle of Forethought, the magical stain remover, and before you know it, your life is suddenly transformed and your entire family is dancing around with lunatic smiles on their faces.

Wherever possible, in a small boat or yacht, you should always keep an eye out to see if you can take early action to prevent close quarters situations from developing.

A smart way of doing this is by altering to point just astern of the crossing vessel. As the crossing vessel tracks through, you continuously alter your heading to follow the same aiming point until you get back to your original course: you will by definition pass astern of her without losing too much time or distance from your planned track. When the crossing vessel is on your port side, this can only be done safely if you start when he is far enough away not to be considering altering to starboard himself (probably 5 miles or more).

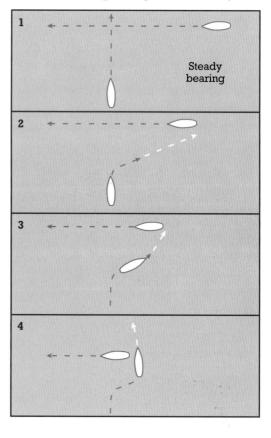

The Swarm Instinct. Don't be alarmed when the entire horizon seems to be full of ships all aiming at you. I have been watchkeeping at sea in one guise or another all my life, and this happens quite regularly. I have concluded that it must be caused by some hormone, still unknown to medical science, that makes me completely irresistible to large steel ships. The trick is to adopt the philosophy of the Russian traveller and always shoot the wolf closest to the sledge, then concentrate on the next one out, and so on.

> **A few thoughts that might help you:**
> * Closer vessels are generally more of an immediate problem than more distant ones. Tick them off one-by-one, starting with the closest.
> * Some will be closing you faster than others: don't bother with ones that are closing very slowly, or opening.
> * If your brain is getting overloaded (this happens to us all occasionally), get crew members to watch individual ships. As a first iteration, if the vessels are moving against the background (clouds, other ships or the land), they are probably not going to hit you, because they are not on a steady bearing. See Section 1 for more details of how to do this.

The manoeuvring rules

I have always thought it a bit strange to call the Manoeuvring Rules the 'Collision Regulations': it's a bit like saying that you will take a Crash Course in driving. That apart, there are a number of important but relatively simple principles about how to keep your vessel safe at sea.

You should be aware that the rules change if you cannot see the other vessel because of restricted visibility. Under these circumstances, it is very much more difficult to know what the other vessel is doing (even if you do have radar – and a lot of people still don't), so the prescribed actions are less subtle, designed to remove all possibility of collision. I have therefore divided this Section into two parts:

* Rules that apply when two vessels are in sight of each other and
* Rules that apply in restricted visibility

They are pretty much mutually exclusive: you can either see the other vessel or you cannot[1].

[1]If you are steaming along the edge of a fog-bank, you may have to deal with some ships using the restricted visibility rules, and others with the 'In Sight of Each Other' rules. In practice, this is not as difficult as it might seem.

Rules that apply to vessels in sight of each other

There are rules that apply between two power driven vessels, or two sailing vessels.

On these basic manoeuvring rules, there is overlaid a rule of precedence (Rule 18) which sets out a 'pecking order' of vessels that suffer from some form of manoeuvring limitation. This rule instructs more manoeuvrable vessels to keep out of the way of vessels that are less manoeuvrable.

Finally, over-riding all of them, there are two special situations where various vessels have priority in any state of visibility. Specifically:
* In a narrow channel or fairway
* In a separation scheme

> **The Convention**
> The convention for manoeuvring at sea is that ships tend to 'drive' on the right. As such, they will through preference pass each other port-to-port.
>
> That means, when approaching from head-to-head, they will have to alter course to starboard to avoid each other. If one chose to alter course to port, it would become very awkward were the other to obey the convention and alter its course to starboard: they would in all likelihood remain on a steady bearing.
>
> Mariners are simple folk, and would prefer not to have too many rules to remember. Recognising this, the rules have been written in such a way that, *in general*, altering course to starboard is preferable to altering course to port as a means of avoiding a collision.
>
> This is not always the case, and every situation needs to be judged on its merits. However, if you find yourself wanting to alter course to port as a means of avoiding a close quarters situation, just pause and think about it for a few seconds before doing so.
>
> In particular, ask yourself the leading question: *'What will happen if I alter course to port and the other guy follows ' the convention' and turns to starboard?'*

Rules that apply to vessels in restricted visibility

In restricted visibility, it is pretty much every man for himself: all vessels are expected to take action to avoid a collision. The aim is to find out as much as you can about a closing contact, whether it is by radar or simply by hearing its sound signal, and then manoeuvre according to some very simple rules.

Once again, there are the two special situations where various vessels have priority:
- In a narrow channel or fairway
- In a separation scheme

Sound signals in restricted visibility differentiate only between power driven vessels and those with a form of manoeuvring restriction. There is, however, no great significance in this. It would be rash for any vessel to assume that it had priority when it could not be certain that the give-way vessel even knew it was there.

So, let's look at the rules. They are not complicated.

Part 1. RULES FOR VESSELS IN SIGHT OF EACH OTHER

In good visibility, the rules for sailing boats are completely different from those that apply to power driven vessels. We will look at power driven vessels first.

Power-driven vessels

There are three types of interaction between power driven vessels. These comprise about 95% of all manoeuvring between vessels at sea. They are:
- The head-on situation
- The crossing situation and
- Overtaking.

Get these under your belt and you are well on the way to making the right decisions at sea in good visibility.

Head-on situation (Rule 14)

The first and simplest of all situations is the head-to-head. Two power-driven vessels are approaching each other head on, or nearly so. What do they do?

Ships drive on the right at sea, so in this case they both turn to the right, making one short blast for their manoeuvring signal as they go. *Piece de gateau*[2].

There is no clear dividing line between a head-on situation and a crossing situation, where two ships are closing each other from the side. This is deliberate: as long as one or both ships turn right ('the convention'), sounding one short blast, there

[2]I was never a star pupil in French lessons at school.

is not going to be a problem. **If one of them tries to go to the left, however, it could be a glorious but expensive mistake!**

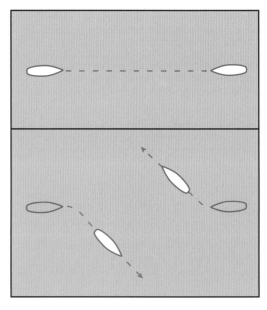

There is one small fly in this ointment, which at the end of the day I will have to leave to your own judgment. What do you do if the other ship, closing from ahead on a reciprocal course, is due to pass close to starboard? In this case, altering to starboard will, in the first instance, *reduce* your passing distance. Altering to port, however, is potentially more risky, because it could put you directly in his path if he altered to starboard.

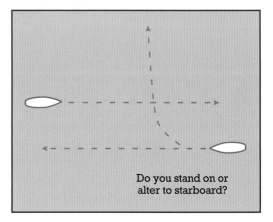

Do you stand on or alter to starboard?

This happened to me once on a fog-bound passage south through the Bay of Biscay, when we encountered a fishing vessel approaching from the south. In the end, because he wasn't altering and I didn't want to cross his bows, he emerged from the fog at about 500 metres, and we passed within about 100 metres of each other, leaving me one rattled officer of the watch. I am still not certain that the fishing boat ever knew we were approaching: when we passed him, I could hear loud music coming from his bridge, and a cheerful figure in his underwear shuffled out onto the bridge wing to give us a sleepy wave.

If you get into a close pass to starboard, you will have to play it as you see it. You either stand on or you turn to starboard. Which one you choose is a matter for your judgment, and will depend on the range of the other vessel at the time, and your prospective passing range. I have put down a few considerations below.

Close pass to starboard:
This is only really a problem if both vessels are on almost parallel courses.
  • If the likely separation is 1000 metres ($^1/_2$ mile) or more, you should just let things go.
  • If the other vessel is set to pass 500 metres or less to starboard, you will need to concentrate a bit. If you have time, you should make a bold alteration to starboard, sounding one short blast. Cross his bows at 90 degrees, and increase speed if appropriate. **But don't even consider this unless you are certain that you have the time and space to do so.**
  • If you are in any doubt about whether you have time, you should stand on and hold your nerve, making sure that you can alter rapidly in either direction as the situation demands, and having as much speed as possible at your disposal.

Crossing situation (Rule 15)

When two power driven vessels are crossing, but on a steady bearing, a collision can only be avoided if one alters course or speed. It is both courteous and sensible that this alteration should result in the give-way vessel passing astern of the other vessel if at all possible. Since we have already established that turning right is the conventional way of avoiding a collision, it is natural that the give-way vessel should be the one which, by turning right, will pass astern of the other vessel.

In practice, it's much simpler than this. Remember it as traffic lights.

If you can see the other guy's green navigation light (ie if you are on his starboard side) you have a green traffic light – so stand on.

If you can see his red navigation light (you are approaching from his port side) you have a red traffic light - so give way.

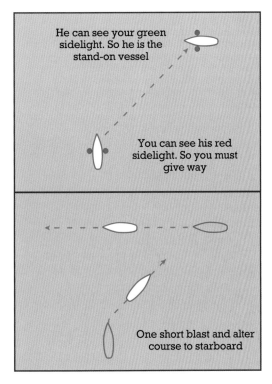

He can see your green sidelight. So he is the stand-on vessel

You can see his red sidelight. So you must give way

One short blast and alter course to starboard

If you are the give way vessel, don't try to cross ahead of the other vessel unless you have stacks of room. Always aim to pass astern.

To make this work, the stand-on vessel should maintain its course and speed: we will look at the question of how long he does so towards the end of the section.

Overtaking situation (Rule 13)

This is one area where 'the convention' does not apply. At sea, the overtaking vessel can go either way.

You are assumed to be overtaking when you are approaching within the arc of the other vessel's stern light. In other words, when you are approaching another vessel from more than $22^1/_2$ degrees abaft his beam. If you are in any doubt about this, you should assume that you are indeed the overtaking vessel.

The logic behind this rule is that no one is forcing you to overtake. So if you do, you do so at your own risk. Therefore,

As an overtaking vessel, you must remain clear of the other vessel until finally past and clear, irrespective of the nature of the two ships concerned.

Even if the vessel being overtaken alters course half-way through the manoeuvre to create a crossing situation, the responsibility for collision avoidance still remains with the formerly overtaking vessel. This is particularly important to bear in mind when on transit through one of the busy separation schemes, or in a narrow channel, when the other vessel might need to alter for its own navigational purposes. You will need to be alert if you are going to remain clear.

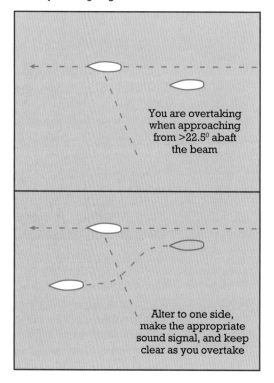

You are overtaking when approaching from >22.5⁰ abaft the beam

Alter to one side, make the appropriate sound signal, and keep clear as you overtake

Sailing vessels (Rule 12)

Sailing boats are a lore unto themselves. However, there are only three rules for general navigation between sailing boats (and about 20,000 that apply when you are racing).

Rule No 1. When two sailing vessels are approaching each other on different tacks, the vessel on the port tack gives way to the one on the starboard tack. A gives way to B.

'Starboard' is a bigger word than 'port'. Might is right. Therefore, the vessel on the starboard tack stands on.

You are on the starboard tack when the wind is coming from your starboard side. To be more precise, it is when the mainsail or, in the case of

a square-rigged vessel the biggest fore-and-aft sail, is set to port.

The 'tack'
In square-rigged sailing vessels, the 'tack' was the rope used to carry the weight of wind in the sail. It was attached to the bottom windward corner of the courses (the lower square sails) and made fast to the ship's side. Thus, with the wind blowing from starboard the weight would be 'on the starboard tack'.
This, incidentally, led to the subsequent use of the word 'tack' for the lower windward corner of the sail (as used in fore-and-aft sails today).

Rule No 2. When two sailing vessels are closing each other on the same tack, the vessel to leeward has right of way. C gives way to D.

Because the windward vessel, it is assumed, has more options at its disposal.

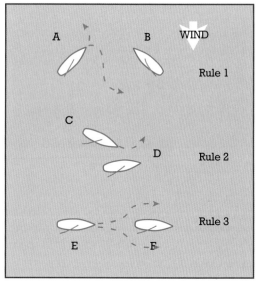

Rule No 3. The overtaking rule applies to sailing boats too. If one sailing boat is approaching another from more than 22.5 degrees abaft the beam, it becomes the overtaking vessel, irrespective of the wind direction or tack. It therefore has to remain clear. E gives way to F.

Responsibilities between different types of vessel: the hierachy (Rule 18)

We have had a look at the most common sort of interactions – those between two power driven vessels, or two sailing vessels. Occasionally, ships meet when one is very obviously less manoeuvrable than the other. In this case, the rules are pretty fair: the more manoeuvrable vessel must 'keep out of the way of' the other.

There are in fact three exceptions to this eminently sensible rule:
- Narrow channels and fairways
- Separation schemes
- Overtaking

The overtaking rule applies at all times. If a vessel Not Under Command decided to overtake a sailing vessel, for instance, nothing written in this rule will prevent him from having to remain clear until finally past and clear. As before, the decision to overtake is his alone, and once he has embarked on that manoeuvre, he is responsible for safety.

We will shortly deal with the special priorities that apply in narrow channels and, to a lesser extent, in separation schemes shortly.

Rule 18 says:

A power driven vessel should keep out of the way of:
- Sailing vessels
- Fishing vessels
- Vessels restricted in their ability to manoeuvre
- Vessels not under command

Sailing vessels should keep out of the way of:
- Fishing vessels
- Vessels restricted in their ability to manoeuvre
- Vessels not under command

Fishing vessels should keep out of the way of:
- Vessels restricted in their ability to manoeuvre
- Vessels not under command

No vessel, with the exception of a vessel Restricted in its Ability to Manoeuvre, or a vessel Not Under Command (who may have no option) should impede the passage of a vessel Constrained By its Draught.

A vessel Restricted in its Ability to Manoeuvre and a vessel Not Under Command are considered to have equal priority and would need to take appropriate action according to their circumstances.

Seaplanes must keep out of everyone's way, although *in extremis* they behave like a power driven vessel.

Let's have a look at this rule in a little more detail.

The pecking order is solely determined by ease of manoeuvre.

Look at the wording that the rules use here. They don't discuss rights of way or give-way and stand-on vessels: they say '*… must keep out of the way of…*'

In other words, a skipper is expected **to think ahead and take early action** to avoid a close-quarters situation or risk of collision occurring with a less manoeuvrable vessel.

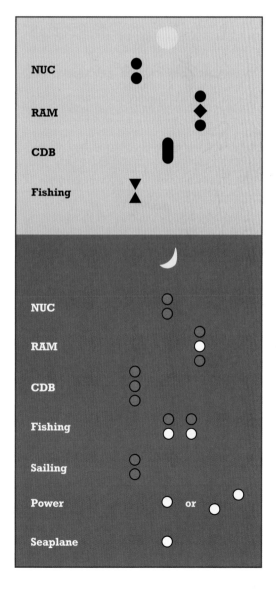

'Power gives way to sail'

In general, I would expect small power boats to give way to sailing vessels.

Large power driven vessels, however, are different. If you think about it, yachtsmen drive just about the most manoeuvrable vessels on the water, and intelligent early action by a sailing boat (or a motor boat for that matter) will often prevent a close quarters situation from occurring[3]. It is therefore quite absurd for a sailing boat to plough on regardless in front of a merchant ship, repeating the old mantra of 'steam gives way to sail'. For a start, you cannot be certain that you have even been seen from the bridge of a large merchant vessel. And secondly, it usually only takes a quick alteration of course or speed by the yacht at an early stage, and the problem just goes away.

That said, the rules are quite specific and in the last analysis – outside narrow channels, separation lanes and overtaking, and avoiding vessels NUC, RAM or constrained by their draught – a power driven vessel that collides with a sailing vessel, of any description, will be held liable. My point is that sailing yachts should recognize the constraints of large merchant vessels and, wherever possible, avoid putting themselves in a position where it becomes an issue.

I remember seeing a photo some years ago. It was a picture of an enormous tanker, under way. In front of it, with the range foreshortened by a telephoto lens, was what looked like a tiny sailing boat. A little speech bubble was coming out of the tanker's bridge saying: 'Sorry... whose right of way do you think it is?'

The two special situations

Narrow Channel or Fairway (Rule 9)

It is not too easy to say what a 'Narrow Channel or Fairway' is. Suffice it to say that large vessels operating in certain channels or fairways, like the approaches to many harbours, will go aground if they move outside the marked channel. And small vessels will do so in commensurately smaller waterways. For that reason, vessels that can only operate in these narrow channels are given specific priority that over-rides other manoeuvring rules. This applies in any condition of visibility.

Specifically (and the first of these is by far the most important):

- **Crossing vessels, sailing vessels and vessels less than 20 m in length must not impede any vessel that is restricted to the channel, no matter which side you are approaching from, and irrespective of the nature of the two vessels involved.**
- When navigating in the channel, you must keep as far to the right as is safe to do.
- Fishing can take place in a narrow channel, but it must not impede the safe passage of ships.
- If at all possible, you should avoid anchoring in a narrow channel. Even if it does have the best fishing on the East Coast!
- Large vessels approaching a blind corner in a narrow channel will often sound one prolonged blast, which should be answered by any other vessel approaching the bend from the other side. If you hear this, you should answer the sound signal if you have a horn loud enough to be heard and take any appropriate action to keep out of the way of the approaching ship.

[3] But think it out first: if you are going to take pre-emptive action, do it early and make it obvious to the other guy what you are doing.

The overtaking rule still applies. However, if vessels need to overtake each other within a narrow channel, there is a sound signal protocol laid down (in the unlikely event that radio communication is unavailable). This is set out in Section 3.

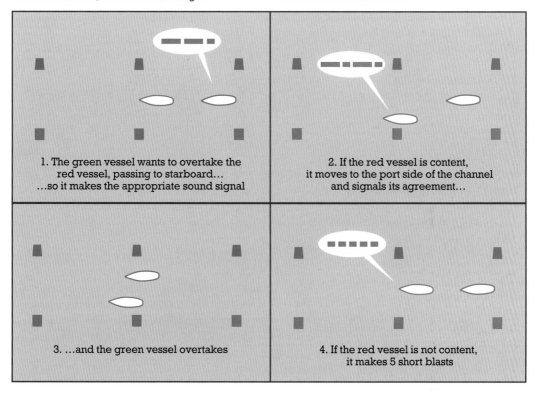

1. The green vessel wants to overtake the red vessel, passing to starboard...
...so it makes the appropriate sound signal

2. If the red vessel is content, it moves to the port side of the channel and signals its agreement...

3. ...and the green vessel overtakes

4. If the red vessel is not content, it makes 5 short blasts

Separation schemes (Rule 10)

Separation schemes are little more than maritime motorways. Because vessels have a little more freedom of manoeuvre than in a narrow channel, the priorities are less restrictive, and large vessels in a scheme are not relieved of any of their normal obligations.

Vessels of less than 20 metres in length, however, or a sailing vessel must not impede the safe passage of a power driven vessel following a traffic lane (Rule 10(j)). This rule over-rides the hierarchy rule (above).

In general, the rules are designed to keep the various traffic flows apart.

Yachts may use the separation lanes but, provided that they are less than 20 metres in length, they may also use the inshore traffic lanes. Take my advice: if you have the opportunity to use the inshore lanes, do so.

However, if you are using the traffic lanes, the rules are exactly like driving along a motorway:
* You must use the appropriate lane for your

direction of travel. The biggest antidote to drowsiness known to man is standing on the bridge of a ship in the Straits of Dover separation scheme at 2am watching a ship come up the scheme towards you against the traffic flow.
* You should as far as possible avoid trespassing on the separation line or separation zone. (Obviously: they are there to keep the opposite traffic flows separated.) You may, however, do so to avoid imminent danger, if you are crossing, or if you are joining or leaving a lane. In addition, fishermen may use the zone if they have to.
* You should either join and leave at the end of the scheme, or enter the lanes at as small an angle as possible.

Don't cross the lanes unless you have to. If you do:
* Make your heading (not your track[4]) as close to 90 degrees to the traffic flow as possible.

* Time your crossing to ensure that, as far as

[4] There can often be a significant difference between heading and track in areas where the tidal stream is substantial. Keep your heading at right angles to the traffic flow so that you maximise your crossing rate.

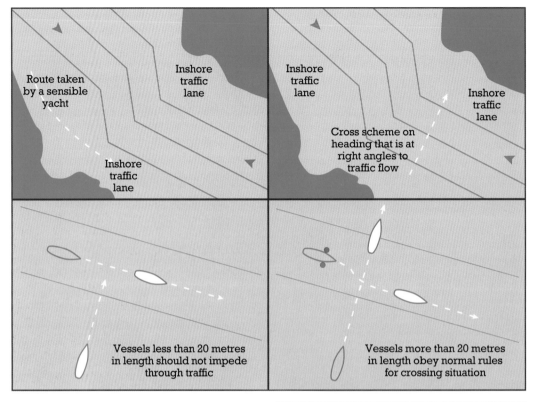

possible, you do not interfere with the through
traffic. You may still have to give way – if you
do, make your alteration early and
unambiguous.

* The normal crossing rules of the road apply to
  vessels longer than 20 metres in good visibility:
  this can make life awkward for vessels
  transiting the scheme and you will need to
  ensure that you do all you can to time your
  crossing to minimise the disturbance.

Inshore traffic zones:
* Can be used at all times by vessels less than
  20 metres in length, sailing vessels and vessels
  engaged in fishing. (A good bet for yachtsmen.)
* Must not be used by other vessels that can
  safely use the separation lane, except when it is
  en route to a destination within the inshore
  traffic zone.

Exemptions:
  Vessels restricted in their ability to manoeuvre
  are exempted from complying with the separation scheme, but only when engaged in:
* Operations for the maintenance of safety of
  navigation in the separation scheme.
* Operations for the laying, servicing or picking
  up of a submarine cable.

I thought it might help if I summarise all these
actions, as they apply to a small sailing vessel
encountering a large fully-manoeuvrable power
driven vessel, in the table below:

Open sea (eg crossing the English Channel)	A small sailing boat should take early action to keep clear of a large power driven vessel through sensible early action. If it does not, the power driven vessel must take avoiding action.
Crossing a separation lane	A sailing vessel, or any vessel less than 20 metres in length, (whether crossing or not) should avoid impeding the passage of any vessel following the separation lane.
Crossing a narrow channel	Crossing vessels must not impede the safe passage of a vessel that is restricted to the narrow channel.
In a narrow channel	Vessels of 20 metres in length or less, whether crossing or not, must not impede the safe passage of a vessel that is restricted to the narrow channel.

Action by the Give-way and Stand-on Vessels (Rules 16 & 17)

Give-way vessel

If you have to give way, the rule is to make your alterarion substantial enough for the officer of the watch in the other vessel to know that you have taken action. Don't nibble at it: a succession of miniscule alterations is probably not going to be visible to the other guy and will make him agitated. Also, a bold alteration of course is almost certainly going to be more visible to the other guy than an alteration of speed: that is why I would almost always advocate an alteration of course, whether or not you choose to alter speed too.

For good measure, to help the other guy understand what is going on, power driven vessels are also obliged to make the manoeuvring sound signals (page 34) when altering course to avoid a collision.

Give the other vessel a good clearance and don't pass close ahead of him ... what would happen if your engine cut out or your sail ripped just as you were passing 100 metres ahead of a large merchant ship?

Stand-on vessel

There are 3 rules for the stand-on vessel:
- **Initially**, maintain course and speed (and keep a very beady look-out).
- You **may take avoiding action** when it becomes apparent that the other vessel is not taking appropriate action.
- You **must act** when you find yourself so close that collision could not be avoided by the action of the give-way vessel alone.

It is frightening when you are the stand-on vessel and you don't know whether the other ship has seen you.

The rules are explicit about the action by the stand-on vessel: it should maintain its course and speed ... but for how long?

The stand-on vessel should keep going *until it is apparent that the give-way vessel is not taking the appropriate action*. For a big merchant ship, my personal chicken factor is something in the order of 1.5 - 2 miles, by which time my nerve normally gives out and I take action myself. This decision is of course entirely up to you, and will depend on your manoeuvrability and speed in comparison to that of the other vessel.

It is also very much up to you what action you take, but unless there is very good reason to do so, **don't alter to port for a vessel on your port side**. The very simple reason for this is that if you alter to port and he suddenly looks out of his window, spots you and grabs the steering control, he will always alter to starboard ... and you will collide.

One 'escape manoeuvre' that I have found useful in these circumstances is to alter right round to starboard and put the other vessel astern. Slow down or speed up as necessary. That way, you can control his closing speed, giving yourself more thinking time and you can easily alter either way if circumstances dictate.

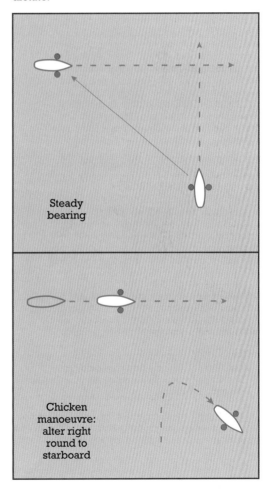

Steady bearing

Chicken manoeuvre: alter right round to starboard

Finally, if things have got so bad that a collision can't be avoided by the give-way vessel alone, the rules give you carte blanche to do anything necessary to avoid a collision. Good luck: tell me about it in the bar one day.

Part 2. RULES FOR VESSELS IN RESTRICTED VISIBILITY (Rule 19)

These are very simple. There are just 3 rules that apply in restricted visibility:

Rule 1. In restricted visibility, **proceed at a safe speed.**

Once again, no-one is going to tell you what a safe speed is, but in my mind it is exactly the same thought process as driving down the motorway: how fast do you drive in fog, or in heavy traffic, or when you are being blinded by the headlights of oncoming traffic? How well can your car manoeuvre? How bumpy is the road? Some of the points that affect 'safe speed' are set out in Rule 6, but if you read them, you will see that it is all really common sense. The big issue is that you should make a realistic assessment of conditions and then set your speed accordingly. If you get it wrong, it is a long way to swim!

Rule 19 also encourages a power driven vessel to '... *have her engines ready for immediate manoeuvre.*'

If you are in a sailing boat and the fog comes down, I would urge you very seriously to consider motoring[5]. It will be noisier, of course, but you will be able to power your way out of trouble very much more easily.

Rule 2. If you detect another vessel on radar and you believe that a risk of collision exists, you should take early avoiding action with two over-riding considerations in mind:

* Don't alter to port for any vessel forward of the beam (except when overtaking).
* Don't alter towards a vessel on your beam or abaft it.

With an operational radar in fog, the only time that you would consider altering to port is when you are being approached by a vessel on your starboard quarter (Example B). On all other occasions you would alter to starboard. How far you turn is up to you, but I should generally make it fairly substantial so that you can be confident that you have sorted out the problem (Example A). There is no 'stand-on' and 'give-way' vessel in fog. The reason for this is that you don't know if the other vessel has radar, or whether he has even detected you. So it is incumbent on everyone – even vessels with manoeuvring restrictions - to do what they can to avoid a collision.

Rule 3. If you don't have an effective radar, and you hear the fog signal of another vessel forward of the beam, you should reduce your speed to the minimum that maintains steerage way unless you can guarantee that a risk of collision does not exist. If necessary, stop altogether until you are sure that it is safe.

The bottom line in fog is to be very, very careful. If you have radar, keep a continuous watch if you can, and try to make sure that you have bearing movement on a contact before it gets too close. If you don't have radar, know which way the prevailing shipping is coming from and don't go any faster than the ambient conditions permit.

The two special situations

Even in restricted visibility, the particular exemptions that apply in Narrow Channels and Fairways, and Separation Schemes, are still valid. These are probably some of the most tricky areas of water to navigate at the best of times, and if you are planning to negotiate them in fog, take very great care.

Overtaking

This is one occasion when the overtaking rule does not apply: if someone is passing up your side in fog, can you be confident that he is aware that you are there, and so will take responsibility for keeping out of your way? No. So don't make any assumptions. Clearly, if you are overtaking someone in restricted visibility, you would want to do everything possible to keep out of the way of other vessels.

---

[5] This will of course mean that you would change your sound signal from that of a sailing boat to a power driven vessel.

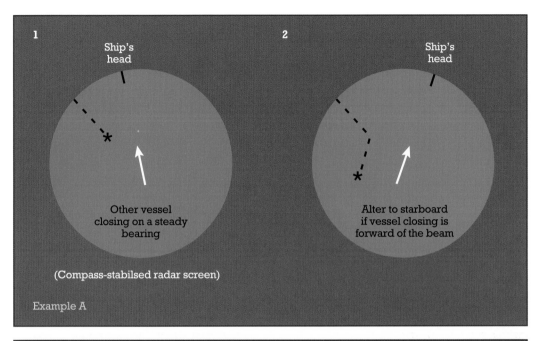

1

Ship's head

Other vessel
closing on a steady
bearing

(Compass-stabilsed radar screen)

Example A

2

Ship's head

Alter to starboard
if vessel closing is
forward of the beam

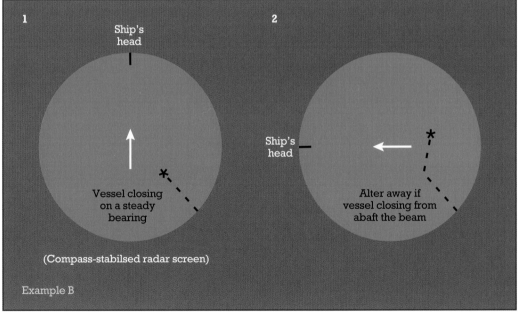

1

Ship's head

Vessel closing
on a steady
bearing

(Compass-stabilsed radar screen)

Example B

2

Ship's head

Alter away if
vessel closing from
abaft the beam

5 Some examples

Head-on situation between two power driven vessels

Applies when vessels can see each other

When two power driven vessels are meeting on reciprocal or nearly reciprocal courses so as to involve risk of collision each shall alter her course to starboard so that each shall pass on the port side of the other. (Rule 14).

One or both vessels alter to starboard and sound one short blast

Don't mess around with niceties here: this is when two vessels have the highest closing rate – and the skippers have the least time to think

Even if you are only approximately in a head-to-head, turn to starboard, sound one short blast, and clear out. The greatest effect that you can have is to turn to a course that is at right-angles to the other vessel: clearly this is only necessary if you are very close, or if you think that he has not seen you.

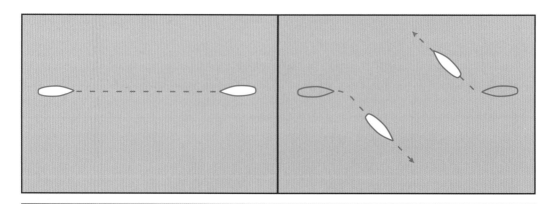

Power driven vessels crossing (you are the give-way vessel)

The vessel with the other on her starboard side gives way and shall, so far as the circumstances admit, avoid crossing ahead of the other vessel. (Rule 15)

The give-way vessel should take early and substantial action to keep clear. (Rule 16)

Provided that the give-way vessel is taking adequate action, the stand-on vessel should maintain course and speed. (Rule 17)
You: turn to starboard and sound 1 short blast.

Other vessel: stand on and monitor the situation.

*Some people get quite confused about who gives way. It is all quite simple – remember **traffic lights.***
If you can see the other guy's green light, you stand on.
If you can see his red light you give way …
by day or night.

If you have to give way, do it early and in a way that cannot be confused by the other vessel. Speeding up from 5 – 6 knots is not really

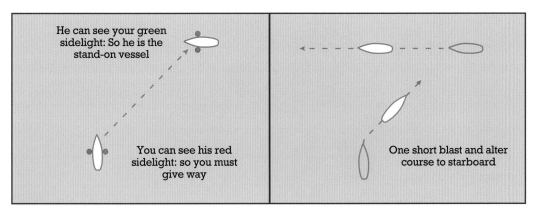

Speeding up from 5 – 6 knots is not really 'substantial action to keep clear'.

If you are keen not to lose too much ground, one trick is to come round early to point (say 10°) behind his stern, and to continue tracking this point as he passes by. When

he crosses your original track, you resume your passage. He will be in no doubt that you are taking action, and you will be able to pass a prudent distance from his stern (and smell what he is cooking for supper into the bargain!).

Power driven vessels crossing in sight of each other (you are stand-on vessel) and the other ship does not give way

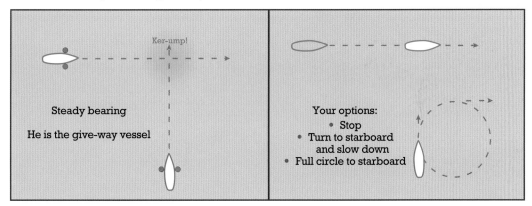

A vessel the passage of which is not to be impeded remains fully obliged to comply with the Rules of this part when the two vessels are approaching each other so as to involve a risk of collision. (Rule 8(f)(ii))

This refers to two rules that apply when vessels can see each other:

The stand-on vessel may take action by her manoeuvre alone when it becomes apparent that the give-way vessel is not taking action. (Rule 17(a)(ii))

And

When from any cause, the vessel required to keep

her course and speed finds herself so close that collision cannot be avoided by the action of the give-way vessel alone, she shall take action as will best aid to avoid collision. (Rule 17(b))

You: Depends on circumstances.
- You may just stop.
- Or you could do a 'retiring turn' – i.e. turn to starboard (1 short blast), and put him on your starboard quarter, or astern. At the same time, adjust speed as necessary.
- One option would be to continue round to starboard in a full 360° turn, by which time he should no longer be a problem.

Other vessel: wake up and alter course to starboard (1 short blast).　▶

This is quite a common situation when you are crossing the English Channel. In many respects it is not surprising that the odd merchant ship just ploughs on, given the number of yachts at sea nowadays.

Do NOT be tempted to turn to port unless you have very good reason: if you do, and he suddenly alters to starboard (as he should) you may find yourself very badly placed.

In any case, keep a really beady eye open for any alterations in his heading.

When should you alter? If you are in any doubt, do it earlier rather than later in a yacht, but I am afraid that you will have to work this out for yourself. In normal circumstances, I would expect to take action myself as the range closes to about 2 miles. This does, however, depend on closing speed, manoeuvrability, etc.

You are overtaking another vessel

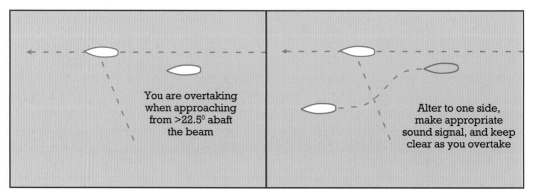

You are overtaking when approaching from >22.5⁰ abaft the beam

Alter to one side, make appropriate sound signal, and keep clear as you overtake

Only applies when vessels can see each other

… any vessel overtaking any other shall keep out of the way of the vessel being overtaken. (Rule 13(a))

Any subsequent alteration of the bearing between the two vessels shall not make the overtaking vessel a crossing vessel within the meaning of these Rules or relieve her of the duty of keeping clear of the overtaken vessel until she is finally past and clear. (Rule 13(d)).

You: Alter course to starboard or port, making

one or two short blasts, as appropriate. Remain clear of the other vessel until you are satisfied that you are 'finally past and clear'.

Other vessel: The overtaken vessel is under no obligation and can alter as appropriate or necessary.

The 'overtaking rule' applies whenever vessels are in sight of each other: in open water, narrow channels and separation lanes.

It applies to any vessel (including sailing boats), even those of reduced manoeuvrability.

Sail and power

Only applies when vessels can see each other

(Rule 18(a)). Except where Rules 9, 10 and 13 otherwise require, a power driven vessel shall keep out of the way of:
• A vessel not under command
• A vessel restricted in its ability to manoeuvre
• A vessel engaged in fishing
• A sailing vessel

Rule 9 applies to narrow channels
Rule 10 to traffic separation schemes
Rule 13 is the overtaking rule.

When the chips are down, **a fully-manoeuvrable power driven vessel must keep clear of any sailing vessel,** except when being overtaken by it.

In practice, however, **a small sailing vessel should take early and positive action to avoid a close quarters situation with any large power driven vessel,** irrespective of this rule. Quite simply, you cannot rely on the fact that it can or will take avoiding action – or even that he has seen you.

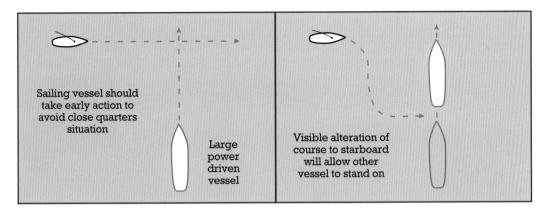

I would expect a small motor boat to keep clear of sailing boats almost always (a small motor boat is, after all, just about the most manoeuvrable vessel on the water).

I would expect a large sailing vessel to exert its priority to a greater extent.

Don't push your luck in a small sailing boat. In general, yachtsmen should avoid putting

themselves in a position where they embarrass large ships.

If you do take action yourself in a sailing boat, remember to do it early and to make any alteration of course large enough for the other vessel to be in no doubt that you are taking the avoiding action.

Sailing boats are under no obligation to make a manoeuvring sound signal (1, 2 or 3 short blasts).

Crossing a separation scheme where there is an appreciable tidal stream

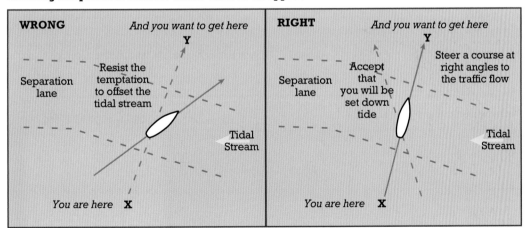

Applies in any condition of visibility

A vessel shall, so far as practicable, avoid crossing traffic lanes but if obliged to do so shall cross on a heading as nearly as practicable at right angles to the direction of traffic flow. (Rule 10(c))

Note the first bit: as far as possible, you should avoid crossing a separation scheme. Period. Believe me, it is not nice trying to get across some of the busier schemes. It's a bit like a tortoise

trying to cross a motorway: it involves a high level of stress and your acceleration is not always up to the job.

The words 'on a heading' are a recent addition to the rules to emphasise that your job is to get across and clear as fast as possible. This will take a little bit of navigational planning in places where there is a strong transverse tidal stream. Still, look on the bright side: your navigator will almost certainly mess it up, and will be forced to buy a round of drinks when you arrive in France.

Meeting another vessel in a separation scheme: crossing situation

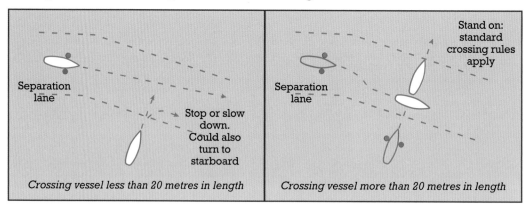

Crossing vessel less than 20 metres in length | Crossing vessel more than 20 metres in length

Applies in any condition of visibility

A vessel of less than 20 metres in length or a sailing vessel shall not impede the safe passage of a power driven vessel following a traffic lane.

Crossing vessel:
* If you are in a small boat or a sailing boat, make sure that you get your timing right!
* If, however, you get caught out and have to take avoiding action, alter to starboard for a vessel crossing from your starboard side. For a vessel crossing from your port side, much will depend on the navigation & traffic situation. You might, however, consider altering to starboard to parallel his course and letting him pass you.
* If you are in a power driven vessel longer than 20 metres, the standard crossing rules apply.

Other vessel:
* Stand on if the crossing vessel is less than 20 metres in length or a sailing vessel... but watch very carefully.
* Apply normal crossing rules for the prevailing visibility if the vessel is longer than 20 metres, or in restricted visibility.

There are a myriad of things to consider here: the navigational constraints of a big ship may well be severe. You will need to keep a close eye on navigation yourself, and indeed on any other traffic that might pose a problem in your vicinity.

Take it steadily and think clearly. Ideally, don't attempt to cross a busy separation scheme in the first place: yachting is meant to be pleasure!

Crossing a narrow channel

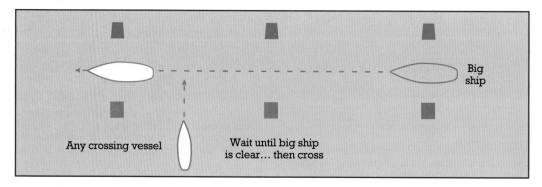

Applies in any condition of visibilty

(Rule 9(b)). A vessel of less than 20 metres in length or a sailing vessel shall not impede the passage of a vessel which can safely navigate only within a narrow channel or fairway.

(Rule 9(d)). A vessel shall not cross a narrow channel or fairway if such a crossing impedes the passage of a vessel which can safely navigate only within such channel or fairway. The latter vessel may use the sound signal prescribed in Rule 34(d) if in doubt as to the intention of the crossing vessel.

Crossing vessel. Stay to one side until the vessel navigating in the channel is past and clear. Then cross. Do not impede the other vessel.

Vessel in the channel. If everyone in the world was sensible, you would be able to stand on and relax. In the real world, you should stand on and trust no one. If in any doubt, sound 5 short blasts.

Small yachts, whether crossing a narrow channel or making a passage along them, must always give way to a vessel that can only navigate within a narrow channel. Rule 9(a) suggests that, in any case, if a channel is narrow, vessels should do everything they can to make room by navigating as far to the starboard side of the channel as is 'safe and practicable'.

Even bigger craft (longer than 20 m) are prohibited from crossing a narrow channel if that will cause embarrassment to a vessel that is constrained to travel along the channel. The 'signal prescribed in Rule 34(d) is five short blasts, meaning: 'Keep out of my way, please'.

Don't forget: in just about every case that I can think of where this rule applies, there will be a common VHF frequency that you can use if you are in doubt. If you are concerned, do not hesitate to call up the controlling authority or the other vessel and discuss the best way to handle the situation. It is a good precaution in busy waters to have a VHF set that you can use in the wheelhouse or cockpit.

Approaching a blind corner in a narrow channel

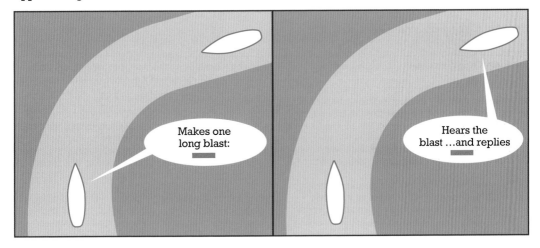

Only applies when vessels can see each other

(Rule 9(f)). A vessel nearing a bend or an area of a narrow channel or fairway where other vessels may be obscured by an intervening obstruction shall navigate with particular alertness and caution and shall sound the appropriate signal prescribed in Rule 34(e).

Rule 34(e). A vessel nearing a bend or an area of a channel or fairway where other vessels may be obscured by an intervening obstruction shall sound one long blast. Such signal shall be answered with a prolonged blast by any approaching vessel that may be within hearing around the bend or behind the intervening obstruction.

A small yacht is probably manoeuvrable enough to be excused the necessity of making the sound signal in anything but the most restricted

waterways. However, you are quite likely to find yourself in a narrow shipping channel where a big ship can't see round the corner properly and makes this sound signal.

It is quite common to hear ferries making one prolonged blast (4 – 6 seconds) in Portsmouth Harbour as they leave the ferryport.
• Large vessels should answer with a prolonged blast and ease over to starboard.
• Small craft hearing this signal should ensure that they clear the channel as quickly as is practical in order to provide room for the big ship to pass. By the time he comes round the corner and can see then next leg of the channel, he will have precious little time to manoeuvre to avoid other shipping.

If either vessel is in any doubt about what is happening, it should make 5 short blasts (Rule 34(d)) and, where possible, communicate on VHF.

Meeting a tow

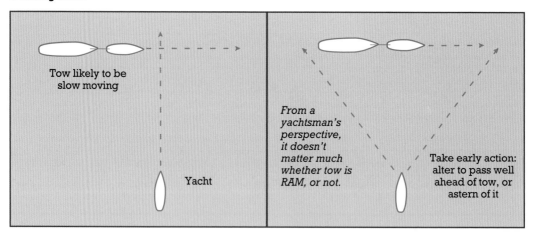

Tow likely to be slow moving

Yacht

From a yachtsman's perspective, it doesn't matter much whether tow is RAM, or not.

Take early action: alter to pass well ahead of tow, or astern of it

Applies when ships are in sight of each other

(Rule 3(g)). The term 'vessel Restricted in her Ability to Manoeuvre' means a vessel which from the nature of her work ... is unable to keep out of the way of another vessel. This shall include...

... A vessel engaged in a towing operation such as severely restricts the towing vessel and her tow in their ability to deviate from their course.

You:
* If at all possible, do not force the tow to give way to you. Take early action to keep out of his way.
* However, if the tow has not declared itself to be RAM, it is obliged to react as a power driven vessel, taking any appropriate action.
* If the vessel has declared itself to be RAM, you must stay clear.

Tow:
* If not RAM, react as a normal power driven vessel, recognising that a tow will almost certainly slow down manoeuvring and restrict the available speed for collision avoidance.

* If you have declared yourself RAM, stand on and watch the situation.

From the point of view of the rules, however, a tow is treated just like any other power driven vessel unless it is showing RAM shapes or lights. The towing lights and shapes are there merely to indicate what is going on , and how far the tow extends.

Practically speaking, I have yet to encounter a tow that is not in some way hampered in its manoeuvrability - try towing another yacht for an hour or two if you don't believe me. Besides, at a distance it is sometimes difficult to make out RAM shapes.

In general, therefore, yachtsmen are well advised to make a small early alteration of course and keep well clear. In this, we are quite fortunate because I have yet to see any tow that speeds along at more than about 4 knots so you should be able to give it a good offing without creating a major drama.

In restricted visibility, a tow is accorded no special privileges, whether it is RAM or not.

Two sailing vessels meeting on opposite tacks

Applies when ships are in sight of each other

(Rule 12(a)). When two sailing vessels are approaching one another, so as to involve risk of collision, one of them shall keep out of the way of the other as follows:
(i) When each has the wind on a different side, the vessel which has the wind on the port side shall keep out of the way of the other.

The course of action by the give-way vessel

depends entirely on circumstances.
  If possible, it is courteous to go downwind of the stand-on vessel and avoid passing too close ahead.
The skipper of the stand-on vessel traditionally stands in the cockpit, shaking his fist and shouting **'STARBOARD'** at the top of his voice. Meanwhile, the skipper of the give-way boat stands defiantly in his cockpit, staring at the other boat and muttering **'IDIOT!'** under his breath. It's all a lot of fun.

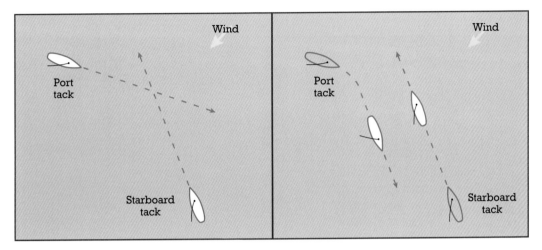

Remember:
You are the stand-on vessel if you are on the starboard tack. And you are on the starboard tack if the wind is blowing from the starboard side (more accurately, if the mainsail is set to port).

Sailing vessels are not obliged to make manoeuvring sound signals, although they are not prohibited from doing so either. That said, I can't recall ever hearing one sounded by a sailing boat in a whole lifetime on the water, but that doesn't mean that you should not do so if you wish.

The important thing in all this is to keep a good lookout. There are a lot of sails obscuring your view and if you react early you will generally get away with only a slight alteration of course, limiting the amount that you will need to diverge from your course or adjust your sails.

Two sailing vessels meeting on the same tack

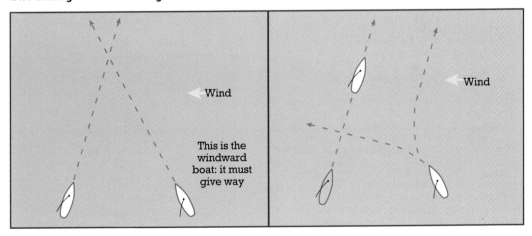

Applies when ships are in sight of each other

(Rule 12(a)). When two sailing vessels are approaching one another, so as to involve risk of collision, one of them shall keep out of the way of the other as follows:
(ii) When each has the wind on the same side, the vessel which is to windward shall keep out of the way of the vessel to leeward.

In other words, the one that is more close-hauled has right of way.
For the give-way vessel, this generally means no more than hardening up a little. At worst, you might have to tack to get out of his way.

As above, there is no obligation for a sailing vessel to make a manoeuvring sound signal.

Restricted visibility. Vessel closing on radar (1)

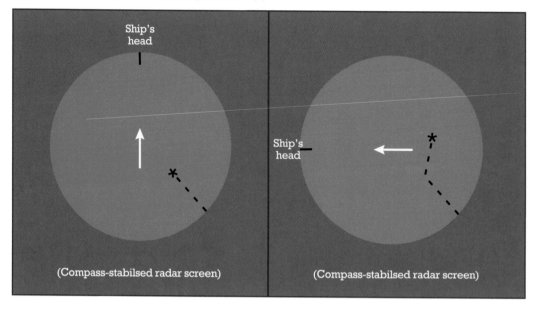

Applies in restricted visibility

(Rule 19(d)). Any vessel which detects by radar alone the presence of another vessel shall determine if a close quarters situation is developing and/or risk of collision exists. If so, she shall take avoiding action in good time, provided that when such action consists of an alteration of course, so far as possible the following shall be avoided:
(ii) an alteration of course towards a vessel abeam or abaft the beam.

In this example, the radar is stabilised on north.

You detect a vessel closing you on your starboard quarter. It must therefore be moving faster than you and converging on your track.

Bear in mind that the overtaking rule does not apply in restricted visibility: if you could see the other vessel it would probably apply here, but in fog where you cannot be certain that the other vessel has detected you, you must always take responsibility for collision avoidance yourself.

In this case, you should alter course to port to increase the passing distance.

There are, of course no manoeuvring sound signals in restricted visibility, as they would be easy to confuse with the fog signals.

Restricted visibility. Vessel closing on radar (2)

Applies in restricted visibility

(Rule 19(d)). Any vessel which detects by radar alone the presence of another vessel shall determine if a close quarters situation is developing and/or risk of collision exists. If so, she shall take avoiding action in good time, provided that when such action consists of an alteration of course, so far as possible the following shall be avoided:
(i) an alteration of course to port for a vessel forward of the beam, other than for a vessel being overtaken.

In this example also, the radar is stabilised on north. This is what the radar looks like in the other ship of the previous example (assuming that the first ship does not alter).

He will be able to work out that he is converging on the other vessel's track and slowly over-hauling it.

Rule 19(d)(i) rightly prohibits him from altering to port (which in the event would merely make matters worse, given the likely action of the other vessel). This vessel should alter to starboard and watch the radar contact track down the port side.

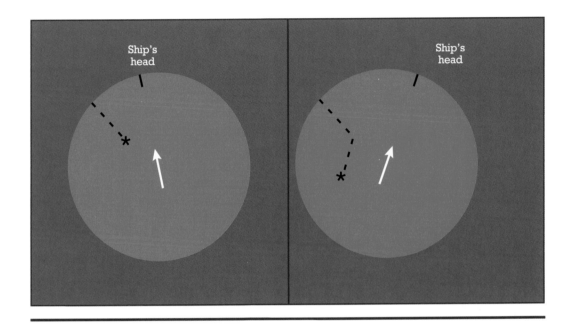

Restricted visibility. No operational radar. Foghorn heard

Applies in restricted visibility

(Rule 19(e)). Except where it has been determined that a risk of collision does not exist, every vessel which hear apparently forward of her beam the fog signal of another vessel, or which cannot avoid a close quarters situation with another vessel forward of her beam, shall reduce her speed to the minimum at which she can be kept on course. She shall if necessary take all her way off and in any event navigate with extreme caution until danger of collision is over.

If you hear another foghorn abaft your beam, keep going. It may be prudent to adjust your course sometimes in order to give greater separation, but on the whole the more you press on the greater the range of the other vessel.

If you hear another foghorn forward of your beam, and you are not absolutely certain that it is not a problem, you should slow down to the minimum at which you have control. If really worried, just stop. Remember that, even if you have radar and you can correlate the bearing of a contact with that of the foghorn, there may be a second vessel on that bearing that you are not picking up on radar. Rule 7(c) says: 'Assumptions shall not be made on the basis of scanty information, especially scanty radar information'. It is very easy making yourself believe what you desperately want to believe. A good skipper is able to question his judgment, even when under pressure. In fog you must be logical, and your decisions need to be right.

Always keep control of your vessel if you can: it is often better to be moving, but in control of your heading, than stopped. Without reliable radar information, try to get some sense of bearing movement from the foghorn.

Very often (but not always) you will know when you get really close to another vessel because you will be able to hear the background noise of the ship. With luck, though, you should be able to see her by that stage!

6 Lights and shapes for yachts

Lights and shapes are there to help vessels identify each other, and to allow mariners to work out what another ship is doing. To that end, it is really important that you carry the right lights yourself, that they work and that they are properly visible.

At the risk of teaching my grandmother to suck eggs, here are a few tips for getting yourself noticed:

- Always service your navigation lights over the winter. Make sure that you have the correct wattage bulbs installed, and that you carry spares.
- Check that your lights are visible over the proscribed arcs, and that they are not blanked out by liferafts, etc. Actually walk or row round the boat and look at them!
- Before setting out, check that your navigation lights work, and have a system of rechecking them periodically during the passage. I once spent 20 minutes in a frigate in Singapore Harbour without lights at night (before they were found to be faulty), and believe me that is scary.
- When you change from sail to power, you have to burn a steaming light – don't be lazy: do it. By the same token, the downward pointing triangle, showing that you are actually under power, is a useful indicator to other mariners. Put it up out of courtesy to them.
- You can sometimes use discretion over the anchor ball. If you are in an area that is likely to be used by other craft on passage it is probably worthwhile, but in a secluded anchorage it may be unnecessary.
- However, the anchor light is more valuable. Firstly, it helps other people coming into an anchorage at night know where you are. Secondly, it is invaluable for finding your way back from the pub!

Lights that you need for your yacht:

Sailing boats. (Rule 25)

Sailing boats must show sidelights and a stern light when underway.

If less than 20 m in length, they may combine this into a single combined lantern at or near the top of the mast where it can best be seen.

If less than 7 m in length, they should if possible show one or other of these light combinations. If not, they should have a white torch that can be used to prevent a collision.

Sailing boats may, in addition to sidelights and stern light, show two all-round masthead lights, red over green, but not if you are showing a combined lantern.

Tips
In practice, the red over green [just the same as traffic lights] is only used on a few big sailing boats, when it can help with identification. You don't see it very often.

*Note that a sailing boat with an engine turns into a power driven vessel the moment the engine is used for propulsion, whether you have sails up o r not. For this reason, most sailing boats are equipped with two sets of lights: those for sailing and those for motoring. **They are different.***

- *When under power, they need a steaming light, sidelights and a stern light.*
- *When under sail, either side lights and a stern light, or a combined lantern.*

The combined masthead lantern should not be used when under power (it is very confusing for other mariners).

If your boat is less than 7 m in length, don't rely on a torch unless it is absolutely unavoidable: install proper navigation lights.

Stern   Port side   Bow

Sidelights & sternlight only – no masthead light

Under 20m may have combined masthead lantern (red/green/white) with no other lights.

(Rare) A yacht may carry an all-round red over green, plus side and stern lights

A sailing yacht when motor sailing shows the same lights as a power vessel. So engine on, masthead lights on.

Motor boats and sailing boats under power (Rule 23)

Assuming that you are not one of the fortunate few who own a motor boat greater than 50 m in length[1] (in which case you will almost certainly be employing a professional skipper to take care of these small details on your behalf), you will need the following lights for your boat:

- Masthead light
- Stern light
- Sidelights

However, if your boat is less than 12 metres in length, you may show:

- An all-round white light (masthead light and stern light combined)
- Side lights

Finally, if your vessel is less than 7 metres in length, you may show:

- An all-round white light
- Where practical, sidelights

Stern   Port side   Bow

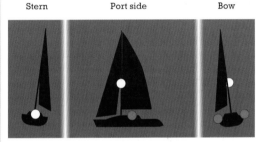

Under 50 m masthead light - sidelights and sternlight.

Under 12 m may show all-round white light (instead of masthead light and sternlight) + sidelights.

Under 7 m and speed under 7 knots may show all-round white light only.   ▶

[1] Clearly, if your boat is over 50 metres in length, you will have two masthead steaming lights.

Tips:
If your boat is less than 7 metres in length, I have some important advice: the great majority of mariners are not telepathic. Therefore, wherever possible, show sidelights – it will keep you and your crew safer, dryer and a lot happier.

And what about your dinghy? (Rules 23 and 25)

Your little inflatable will almost certainly be used at night, hopelessly overcrowded and full of slightly tipsy[2] bonhomie as you make your way back from the pub. It is too late by then to wish that you had brought a torch, or switched on your anchor light, or taken the phone number of the barmaid. I can't offer you much advice about the latter point, but I would advise you always (even if it is broad daylight when you leave the boat) to pack a good reliable torch and to leave the anchor light burning.

The rules say:

* When under power, a dinghy should be considered to be a power-driven vessel of less than 7 m in length. i.e. it should carry a single all-round white light.
* When under oars it should, where possible, exhibit the lights of a sailing vessel, i.e. sidelights and a stern light. However, if that is not possible it should have at hand a white torch or lantern that the crew can exhibit in sufficient time to prevent a collision.

Not many of us have navigation lights on our inflatables. None, in fact. So make absolutely certain, however you intend to propel your dinghy, that you have a strong and reliable torch with you at night. If you have to use it, don't blind the skipper of the oncoming vessel – aim it just off his eye-line, but make sure that he is fully aware of where you are and what direction you are heading in.

Visibility of lights (Rule 22)

Vessels 12 – 20m in length:

Masthead light	3 miles
Sidelights	2 miles
Stern light	2 miles

Vessels less than 12m in length:

Masthead light	2 miles
Sidelights	1 mile
Stern light	2 miles

A light of 25 watts should provide at least 3 miles visibility in a white light and at least 2 miles in a coloured light.

Shapes to carry on your yacht

In reality, you will only need two shapes for a sailing boat: a black ball and a black cone.

A motor boat will just need a black ball.

A sailing boat that is under power should, by day, show a black cone, apex downwards.

The black ball should be hoisted, by day, in the fore part of the vessel, where it can best been seen, when at anchor.

In vessels greater than 20 m in length, the shapes should be:

* Ball   >0.6 m in diameter
* Cone   >0.6 m in diameter
            Length equal to height

Vessels of less than 20 m in length may have smaller shapes, but of a size commensurate with the size of the vessel.

And finally, don't forget the foghorn!

No size is stipulated but Boissier's first rule of foghorns is this:

THE LOUDER THE BETTER

What sounds embarrassingly loud in the chandlery is often no more that a rather sad grunt at sea. Remember, the only reason that you carry a foghorn is to be heard. That is its sole purpose in life: if it can't even manage that, you might as well chuck it away and make space for something useful.

If it's aerosol-powered, buy a couple of spare cylinders while you are at it (and try to remember where you stow them).

---

[2] In both senses of the word.

7 Distress signals

Every book that I have ever read about survival at sea has a bit about how they see ships only a few miles away that steam past and over the far horizon without noticing them. That is why you carry flares and why the Rules go to so much trouble to prescribe a range of distress signals that you can use. They are all laid out in Annex IV to the Rules. A distress signal means just one thing: 'I am in distress and I need assistance.'

They are used by people asking to be rescued. The distress signals do not, under any circumstances, mean 'I have a box of time-expired flares that I am shooting off for my wife's birthday.' Or even, in the case of the raising arms signal, 'I am an aerobics teacher, doing my early-morning stretching exercises.' If you see them, or if your hear them, they are for real.

We all know 'SOS' and quite a lot of people are aware of 'Mayday', but did you realise that the first signal, a gun fired at intervals of about 1 minute, was a distress signal? Or that the continuous sounding of a fog-signalling apparatus meant any more than 'I have a particularly dreadful 4 year-old aboard'? For the sake of all of us who use the sea, get your head around these signals and do, please, take them seriously.

And this brings me to mobile phones. These work 2-3 miles out to sea, maybe more. But that doesn't count as a reliable bit of safety equipment. Sure, use your mobile if all else fails, but your first line of defence is VHF, flares etc.

This is the list of distress signals. There are 15 of them. Try testing each other on the long dull night watches.

1	A gun or other explosive device at intervals of about 1 minute	
2	Continuous sounding of any fog-signalling apparatus	
3	Rockets or shells, throwing red stars, fired one at a time, at short intervals	
4	A signal made by radiotelephony or by any other signalling method consisting of the group ··· ——— ··· (SOS in the Morse Code)	 ▶

5	A signal sent by radiotelephony consisting of the spoken word 'Mayday'	
6	The international code of signals for distress indicated by 'NC'	
7	A signal consisting of a square flag having above or below it a ball, or anything resembling a ball	
8	Flames on the vessel (as from a burning tar barrel, oil barrel, etc)	
9	A rocket parachute flare or hand flare showing a red light	
10	A smoke signal giving off orange-coloured smoke	
11	Slowly and repeatedly raising and lowering arms outstretched to each side	
12	The radiotelegraph alarm signal. (Twelve four-second dashes per minute, set at one-second intervals)	 5 sec
13	The radiotelephone alarm signal. (Alternate tones of 1300 Hz and 220 Hz transmitted on 2182 kHz for a period of 30 to 60 seconds)	 1300 Hz 2200 Hz
14	Signals transmitted by Emergency Position-Indicating Radio Beacons (EPIRBs)	
15	Approved signals transmitted by radiocommunication systems, allowing the full range of GMDSS eqipment to be employed	

8 Buoyage

I thought that I would add just a small section about buoyage. It is not complicated and, with the application of a few brief mnemonics, you will never be in a position to forget your way around at sea again.

Buoys are a country's way of welcoming you to their waters. There are never enough of them, but they are used to mark the safe channels in and out of harbour, and around obstructions. The first thing to remember about buoys is that they are never in a precise spot; they are anchored to the bottom, often with more than one anchor, but they can – and do – drag their anchors on occasions, and even when they have not done so, the slack in the mooring chain allows the buoy to describe a small circle on the surface. Accurate fixing with a buoy is therefore inadvisable.

The next thing to have in the back of your mind is that, even when they have dragged, they are almost never very far out of position; consequently when the navigator of a yacht (or a warship) pops his head up on deck and reports that the buoy has 'clearly been removed', the wise skipper takes a good hard look at his position.

There are two sorts of buoyage in general use:
* The **cardinal system**, where marks are designed to indicate which direction a danger lies in, and therefore which direction is safe for navigation
* The **lateral system**, which is commonly used in navigable channels, with one set of shapes and colours being kept to one side, and another set on the other side.

The cardinal system is consistently applied around the world, although it is more heavily used in Europe than North America. By contrast, there are two similar but distinct forms of lateral buoyage, both of which have been sanctioned by the International Association of Lighthouse Authorities (IALA).

* **Region B** applies to North and South America, Korea, Japan and the Philippines.
* **Region A** applies to all countries in the world that do not fall within Region B.

Buoys can be identified by a number of features: their shape and the shape of their topmarks. They generally have a name or number painted on the side (a dead give-away), sound signals, colour and, very occasionally, a radar transponder.

In addition, there are three other kinds of navigation buoys and marks:

* Safe water marks
* Isolated danger marks
* Special marks

They all have their own distinct characteristics.

THE CARDINAL SYSTEM

The clever thing about the cardinal system is that you don't need to know where you are, or even what harbour you are going into in order to remain safe. That said, it isn't totally idiot-proof because you do need to know what the buoys mean and you also need a functioning compass (or at least a fairly reliable sense of direction).

In essence, the system uses the four cardinal points of the compass (north, south, east and west) to mark an obstruction. The buoys in each quadrant can be distinguished from each other by virtue of their paint scheme, their topmark and their light characteristics. Thus, a 'northerly cardinal mark' lies generally to the north of an obstruction and vessels should pass to the north of it. Not all cardinal marks are buoys; there are a lot of beacons with the same distinctive colouring, topmark and lighting that are designed to fit into this system.

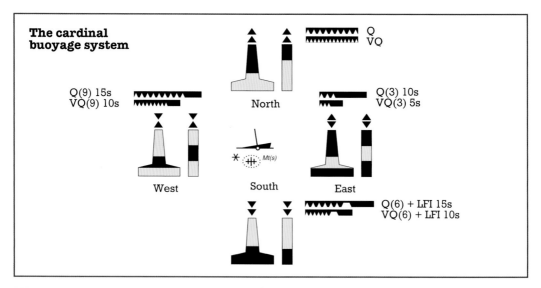

The cardinal buoyage system

How do you remember the cardinal buoys?

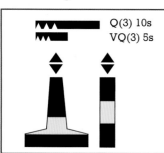

Q(3) 10s
VQ(3) 5s

EAST CARDINAL
Topmark. Looks like a primitive **'E'** with the black shading between the horizontals.
Colours. In the cardinal system the buoys are always yellow and black, and the points on the topmark always point towards the 'black bits'. Thus, this mark is yellow in the middle and black at top and bottom.
Light. All cardinal marks are either Quick Flashing or Very Quick Flashing, and the light is always white. This mark is placed at '3 o'clock' relative to the central obstruction , and so has a group of 3 flashes.

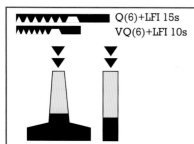

Q(6)+LFl 15s
VQ(6)+LFl 10s

SOUTH CARDINAL
Topmark. Points south (reasonably enough)
Colours. Same system applies as before. The topmark points indicate the 'black bits', so this buoy is black at the base and yellow above.
Light. Sitting at '6 o'clock', this mark has six flashes. However, recognising that most of us navigators are bears of very little brain, the designers thought (correctly) that it would be very easy to confuse 6 flashes of the southerly mark with 9 flashes of the westerly mark. Therefore, they have put a long flash on the end of the shorter pattern to distinguish them.

Q(9) 15s
VQ(9) 10s

WEST CARDINAL
Topmark. Shaped like a **'W'** that has been rotated through 90°. Alternatively, it is often said to look like a **Wineglass**.
Colours. Same system again.
The topmark points indicate the 'black bits', so this buoy is black in the middle and yellow elsewhere.
Light. This is the '9 o'clock' buoy and has nine straight flashes.

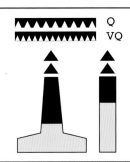

NORTH CARDINAL
Topmark. Both cones point north.
Colours. Same again. The topmark points indicate the 'black bits', so this buoy is black at the top and yellow below.
Light. This is the 'midnight buoy' and it flashes continuously.

THE LATERAL SYSTEM

IALA System A

This system applies to all the world, except North and South America, Korea, Japan and the Philippines. The buoys are distinguished by all the same features as the cardinal system, but they also change shape, depending on which way they should be passed.

In a nutshell, when you are sailing **WITH THE FLOOD TIDE**, you leave the red buoys and marks to port and the green buoys and marks to starboard. The direction of the main flood tidal stream is generally relatively easy to determine, but where there is any ambiguity it is indicated on the chart with the purple arrow symbol.

Lateral marks

Port hand buoys and marks

Direction of buoyage symbol

Starboard hand buoys and marks

Port hand buoys and marks are:
• Can-shaped
• Have cylindrical topmarks
• Are painted red
• Have red lights
• Have even numbering

Starboard hand buoys and marks are:
• Conical in shape
• Have triangular topmarks
• Are painted green
• Have green lights
• Have odd numbering

Modified lateral marks

These are the 'preferred channel marks', that I have never noticed especially but which deserve recognition as part of the system. They tend to be used when a channel divides. You can pass either side, but one side is preferred.

Preferred channel to starboard

Preferred channel to port

IALA System B

Used in North and South America, Japan, Korea and the Philippines.

Is actually very similar to System A, except that you keep the red buoys to starboard when entering harbour and the green buoys to port. The universal mnemonic for this is:

'RED – RIGHT – RETURNING'

There are also preferred channel marks, which are the opposite to IALA System A:

Preferred channel to starboard (when entering harbour)	Preferred channel to port (when entering harbour)
• May have a green light • May be lettered	• May have a red light • May be lettered

Port hand buoys and marks:

• Are painted green
• Are square shaped
• Have odd numbers
• Have green lights

Lateral System (IALAB) as seen entering from seaward

Starboard hand buoys and marks:

• Are painted red
• Buoys can be slant-sided ('nun buoys')
• Daymarks are triangular
• Have even numbers
• Have red lights

Safe water marks

Common to any buoyage system. A safe water mark is normally placed as the outer marker to a conventional buoyage system. It shows safe water all-round.

Topmark. Circular red.
Colour. Vertical stripes: red and white
Light. Gentle rhythm: this is a 'safe' buoy. Isophase, or occulting, or one long flash every 10 seconds.
Or Morse 'A' (• ▬)

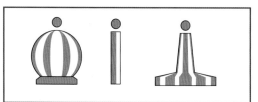

Isolated danger marks

Common to any buoyage system. Mark an isolated danger, normally within a marked navigation channel

Topmark. 2 black balls. You can mess up significantly if you ignore this mark, hence the old 'balls-up' symbol again.

Colour. A sinister red and black: a sort of Cruella de Ville outfit.
Light. Group flashing white (2).

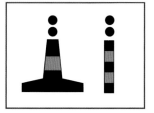

Special marks and buoys

These are not navigation marks, but are used to indicate a particular feature. In the Solent, for instance, all the racing marks are unlit spherical yellow buoys without topmarks.

Topmark. Yellow diagonal cross (if any).
Colour. Yellow.
Light. Yellow (when fitted).
Shape. Any that does not conflict with navigation marks.

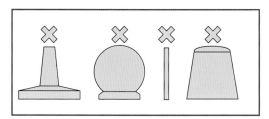

9 The Rules
(from a yachtsman's perspective)

As an ordinary human being, and a yachtsman at that, you will naturally consider this a section to avoid. I know what you mean. However, there is some quite good stuff here, and if you are going to keep yourself and your boat safe, you really do need to have a working proficiency of the rules themselves, not just the lights and shapes. The Merchant Navy and the Royal Navy now insist on a 100% score on Rule of the Road for their bridge watchkeeping officers. You don't need to hit this sort of target in a yacht, but you do need to be absolutely confident that you are doing the right thing.

You can tell when you are getting it wrong and scaring your crew: first your friends will desert you, then your wife refuses to sail with you and at last the dog walks off in disgust.

The rules are really not so bad as all that: take a little time to go through them. I have highlighted the bits that I think yachtsmen ought to be aware of.

Part A – General Rules

Rule 1. Application

(a) These rules shall apply to all vessels upon the high seas and in all waters connected therewith navigable by seagoing vessels.

(b) Nothing in these rules shall interfere with the operation of special rules made by an appropriate authority for roadsteads, harbours, rivers, lakes or inland waterways connected with the high seas and navigable by seagoing vessels. Such special rules shall conform as closely as possible with the rules.

(c) Nothing in these rules shall interfere with the operation of any special rules made by the Government of any state with respect to additional station or signal lights, shapes or whistle signals for ships of war and vessels proceeding under convoy, or with respect to additional station or signal lights or shapes for fishing vessels engaged in fishing in a fleet. These additional station or signal lights, shapes and whistle signals shall, so far as possible, be such that they cannot be mistaken for any light, shape or signal authorised elsewhere under the rules.

(d) Traffic separation schemes may be adopted by the Organisation for the purpose of the rules.

(e) Whenever the government concerned shall have determined that a vessel of special construction or purpose cannot comply fully with the provisions of any of these Rules with respect to the number, position, range or arc of visibility of lights or shapes, as well as to the disposition and characteristics of sound-signaling appliances, such vessel shall comply with such other provisions in regard to the number, position, range or arc of visibility of lights or shapes, as well as to the disposition and characteristics of sound-signaling appliances, as her Government shall have determined to be the closest possible compliance to these Rules in respect to that vessel.

In essence, this rule says two things to yachtsmen:
- *Always do your homework. The rules often get adapted locally, but changes should be published in a good pilot book, and any recent amendments will be distributed in notices to mariners.*
- *Don't be surprised when other vessels don't stick to the rules precisely. The very great majority do, but there will always be exceptions.*

Rule 2. Responsibility

(a) Nothing in these rules shall exonerate any vessel, or the owner, master or crew thereof, from the consequences of any neglect to comply with these Rules or the neglect of any precaution which may be required by the ordinary practice of seamen, or by the circumstances of the case.

(b) In construing and complying with these rules due regard shall be had to all dangers of navigation and collision and to any special circumstances, including the limitations of the vessel involved, which may make a departure from these rules necessary to avoid imminent danger.

If you abide by the Rules, your actions will be

understood and respected by competent mariners, and you will be keeping yourself, your passengers and your crew safe. The Rules cannot cater for every eventuality and there may be times when you have to diverge from the Rules in order 'to avoid imminent danger'.

Things can quite often get a little steamy at sea: complex situations seem to bubble out of thin air at times and as a skipper you will need to sort them out without compromising the safety of your crew or other seafarers. To do this you need to understand the Rules properly, but you also need to have an understanding of the 'the ordinary practice of seamen'. This comes with time and experience – and has nothing (in this context, at least) to do with waterfront ale-houses. The moral is to take it gently to begin with and not to take unnecessary risks until you are genuinely confident that you know what is going on.

If you get it wrong through negligence, you will be held responsible. The seaways round the UK and the US are getting busier each year, and they are being used by ever-larger vessels that have less freedom of manoeuvre. Each year in Portsmouth and the Solent we prosecute a number of ships or boats, together with their skipper and owners, because they acted irresponsibly.

There is a story – probably apocryphal – about a yachtsman who ended up in court after being arrested for obstructing the passage of a vessel constrained by its draught. He had the misfortune, unbeknownst to him, of appearing before a magistrate who was himself an experienced yachtsman, and who knew full well that the defendant had been negligent.
At the appropriate moment, the magistrate leant forward and, peering at the defendant over his pince-nez, asked:
'So how do you plead to this charge?'
'Not guilty, sir' came the inevitable reply.
'Not what?' asked the magistrate, incredulously.
'Guilty, sir' said the defendant.
'That's more like it. Now let's get on with the sentencing.'

Rule 3. General Definitions

Don't be put off by the apparently bureaucratic nature of the wording in the rules: there is, to me at least, something faintly ridiculous about any regulation that kicks off with the words: 'The term 'vessel restricted in her ability to manoeuvre' means a vessel which from the nature of her work is restricted in her ability to manoeuvre…'.

Hang on in there: there are some quite valuable points buried amongst it all.

For the purposes of these rules, except where the context otherwise requires:

(a) The word 'vessel' includes every description of water craft, including non-displacement craft and seaplanes, used or capable of being used as a means of transportation on water.

(b) The term 'power driven vessel' means any vessel propelled by machinery.

(c) The term 'sailing vessel' means any vessel under sail, provided that propelling machinery, if fitted, is not being used.

(d) The term 'engaged in fishing' means any vessel fishing with nets, lines, trawls, or other fishing apparatus which restrict manoeuvrability, but does not include a vessel fishing with trolling lines or other fishing apparatus which do not restrict manoeuvrability.

(e) The word 'seaplane' includes any aircraft designed to manoeuvre on the water.

(f) The term 'vessel not under command' means a vessel which through some exceptional circumstance is unable to manoeuvre as required by these rules and is therefore unable to keep out of the way of another vessel.

(g) The term 'vessel restricted in her ability to manoeuvre' means a vessel which from the nature of her work is restricted in her ability to manoeuvre as required by these rules and is therefore unable to keep out of the way of another vessel.

The term 'vessels restricted in her ability to manoeuvre' shall include, but not be limited to:
(i) A vessel engaged in laying, servicing or picking up a navigation mark, submarine cable or pipeline.
(ii) A vessel engaged in dredging, surveying or underwater operations.
(iii) A vessel engaged in replenishment or transferring persons, provisions or cargo while underway.
(iv) A vessel engaged in launching or recovery of aircraft
(v) A vessel engaged in mineclearance operations
(vi) A vessel engaged in towing operations such as severely restricts the towing vessel and her tow in their ability to deviate from their course.

(h) The term 'vessel constrained by her draft' means a power driven vessel which, because of her draught in relation to the available depth and width of navigable water, is severely restricted in her ability to deviate from the course that she is following.

(i) The term 'underway' means that a vessel is not at anchor, or made fast to the shore, or aground.

(j) The words 'length' and 'breadth' of a vessel mean her length overall and her greatest breadth.

(l) Vessels shall be deemed to be in sight of each other only when one can be observed visually from the other.

(m) The term 'restricted visibility' means any

condition in which visibility is restricted through fog, mist, falling snow, heavy rainstorms, sandstorms, or any other similar causes.

These rules apply to just about anything that floats and can be used for water-borne transport.

Rule 3c is an important one for yachtsmen of the sailing variety. The minute you start your engine and engage the propeller, you become a power driven vessel. Your lights change, your rules change and your obligations change.

Rule 3d. From the perspective of the rules, you do not become a vessel engaged in fishing just by towing a mackerel line over the stern. Vessels authorised to display fishing lights or shapes are, in some fashion, limited in their manoeuvrability. They are also out there to make a living and so, from a yachtsman's perspective, it is courteous to keep out of the way of both fishing boat and outlying gear.

Rule 3f. A vessel will only declare itself not under command if it is virtually powerless to take avoiding action due to some 'unforeseen circumstance'. In other words, there is a major crisis onboard. It may still be making way, but its actions will be unpredictable and there will be a lot of people on the bridge working hard to sort out the problem. Stay clear. The not under command lights and shapes are not a distress signal.

Rule 3g. Vessels restricted in their ability to manoeuvre are also characters that you really don't want to mix with. As a naval officer, I have been engaged in almost every one of these evolutions from time to time. Believe me, there is nothing worse than having a diver under the water when a fast motor boat screams past to see that is going on. Please don't get too close. These vessels are sometimes more manoeuvrable than not under command – but only just. But occasionally, for instance when launching and recovering aircraft, they will be moving very fast. Give them space.

Rule 3h. Vessels constrained by their draught are arguably the most dodgy of the lot. No ship is going to put up these lights and shapes unless she is really very limited in her options. As captain of a nuclear submarine operating out of Plymouth, my tugs would carry the shapes for me – but even that did not stop one enterprising chap in a motor boat with a camera from almost colliding with us in an attempt to get a close-up action photograph. I was too worried even to give him my film-star smile. He appeared in court a week later.

Rule 3k. This is important, since Rules 11 – 18 only apply when vessels are in sight of each other. If you can't see the other guy, for whatever reason – poor visibility or some intervening cliff face – your parameters are different. At times, this can be quite exciting: in patchy visibility you may be working to the 'in sight of each other' rules for one contact, and the 'restricted visibility' rules for another…. Stay flexible: boating would not be so interesting if it was all too simple.

Part B - Steering and Sailing Rules

Section I - Conduct of Vessels in any Condition of Visibility

Rule 4. Application

Rules in this section apply to any condition of visibility.

Rules 5 – 8 determine some of the fundamental practices of maritime safety. There is no rocket science about them: they are simple and intuitive and you should take the time to become familiar with them.

Rules 9 & 10 look after the two special situations – narrow channels and separation schemes – when big ships tend to become nervous. The rules have been beefed up to give them additional safeguards in these circumstances that apply in all states of visibility.

Rule 5. Look-out

Every vessel shall at all times maintain a proper look-out by sight as well as by hearing as well as by all available means appropriate in the prevailing circumstances and conditions so as to make a full appraisal of the situation and of the risk of collision.

How well can you swim?
If you asked any amateur mariner what his most important piece of safety equipment is, he would say GPS, or radar, or his liferaft. If you ask a halfway competent professional seaman, he will say the Mark 1 Eyeball. Don't be seduced in your yacht by a good book, or lunch, or the film star looks of your crew. When you are at sea, someone has to be keeping a thorough and regular lookout. If not, you may well be swimming home!

Rule 6. Safe Speed.

Every vessel shall at all times proceed at a safe speed so that she can take proper and effective action to avoid collision and be stopped within a distance appropriate to the prevailing circumstances and conditions.
In determining a safe speed the following factors shall be among those taken into account:
  (a) By all vessels:
  (i)   The state of visibility;
  (ii) The traffic density including concentrations of fishing vessels or any other vessels;
  (iii) The manageability of the vessel with special reference to stopping distance and turning ability in the prevailing conditions;
  (iv) At night the presence of background light such as from shore lights or from back scatter from her own lights;

(v) The state of wind, sea and current, and the proximity of navigational hazards;

(vi) The draft in relation to the available depth of water.

(b) Additionally, by vessels with operational radar:

(i) The characteristics, efficiency and limitations of the radar equipment;

(ii) Any constrains imposed by the radar range scale in use;

(iii) The effect on radar detection of the sea state, weather and other sources of interference;

(iv) The possibility that small vessels, ice and other floating objects may not be detected by radar at an adequate range;

(v) The number, location and movement of vessels detected by radar;

(vi) The more exact assessment of the visibility that may be possible when radar is used to determine the range of vessels or other objects in the vicinity.

It seems to me that there are two sorts of people in life: sensible people and idiots.
There is nothing in this rule that any ordinary car driver would find strange. The parameters of visibility, traffic density, weather, handling characteristics, etc are all pretty much straight translations of the decision that you make every time you get into your car: how fast should I drive on this piece of road?
If you are a sensible yachtsman – or commercial skipper – this is an instinctive decision, and you do not need me or the Rules to tell you how fast to go. It will just feel right.
If you are an idiot, try your best to leave that side of your character at home when you go out in a boat: it is embarrassing, expensive, and people can (and do) get hurt.

Rule 7. Risk of Collision

(a) Every vessel shall use all available means appropriate to the prevailing circumstances and conditions to determine if risk of collision exists. If there is any doubt such risk shall be deemed to exist.

(b) Proper use shall be made of radar equipment if fitted and operational, including long-range scanning to obtain early warning of risk of collision and radar plotting or equivalent systematic observation of detected objects.

(c) Assumptions shall not be made on the basis of scanty information, especially scanty radar information.

(d) In determining if risk of collision exists the following considerations shall be among those taken into account:

(i) Such risk shall be deemed to exist if the compass bearing of an approaching vessel does not appreciably change;

(ii) Such risk may sometimes exist even when an appreciable bearing change is evident, particularly when approaching a very large

vessel or a tow or when approaching a vessel at close range.

This is another helping of good, basic common sense. There are, however, two issues buried here: firstly that radar is both less accurate and more complex to interpret than visual information – so don't go rushing off using half-baked information when a slightly more meticulous assessment would point you towards a more sensible course of action.

Secondly, at close quarters, you must keep a beady eye on both ends of a big ship. Sure as eggs, if one end is drawing right, and the other is drawing left, there will be a spot in the middle that is on a steady bearing: that is the bit that you will collide with.

The single and complete criterion for risk of collision is that another vessel is closing and that its true bearing (not relative bearing) is not changing.

Rule 8. Action to Avoid Collision

(a) Any action taken to avoid collision shall, if the circumstances of the case admit, be positive, made in ample time and with due regard to the observance of good seamanship.

(b) Any alteration of course and/or speed to avoid collision shall, if the circumstances of the case admit, be large enough to be readily apparent to another vessel observing visually or by radar; a succession of small alterations of course and/or speed should be avoided.

(c) If there is sufficient sea room, alteration of course alone may be the most effective action to avoid a close-quarters situation provided that it is made in good time, is substantial and does not result in another close-quarters situation.

(d) Action taken to avoid collision with another vessel shall be such as to result in passing at a safe distance. The effectiveness of the action shall be carefully checked until the other vessel is finally past and clear.

(e) If necessary to avoid collision or allow more time to asses the situation, a vessel may slacken her speed or take all way off by stopping or reversing her means of propulsion.

(f)

(i) A vessel which, by any of these rules, is required not to impede the passage or safe passage of another vessel shall, when required by the circumstances of the case, take early action to allow sufficient sea room for the safe passage of the other vessel.

(ii) A vessel required not to impede the passage or safe passage of another vessel is not relieved of this obligation if approaching the other vessel so as to involve risk of collision and shall, when taking action, have full regard to the action which may be required by the rules of this part.

(iii) A vessel the passage of which is not to be impeded remains fully obliged to comply with the rules of this part when the two vessels are approaching one another so as to involve risk of collision.

I was a very timid bridge watchkeeper when I first started out.

'Don't mess around,' one of my early captains used to say to me when I proposed some hopelessly inadequate manoeuvre to avoid another ship, 'this is one of the few opportunities that you have in life to make the grand operatic gesture.'

He was right. If you are going to alter for another vessel, provided there is enough water to do so, do it by altering course (which is more immediately obvious to the other guy). Do it early enough for him to tick you off his 'these are the things that I am most anxious about' list, and make sure that the gesture is sufficient, in one bight, to pass at a safe distance. In short, be flamboyant about it!

Even once you have made the gesture, keep an eye on him. How do you know that he has not got a pre-planned course alteration in two minutes time that will set him once again on a steady bearing.

And never forget the option of stopping if you are worried[1]. I quite often turn my boat through 360 degrees (away from a threatening ship) if I am worried about him. This effectively holds my position for a couple of minutes whilst allowing him to get out of my way.

Rule 8(f)(ii) is a little weird. What it is saying refers you to Rule 9, 10 and 18 (Narrow channels, separation schemes and the 'hierarchy rule'. By way of an example, as a yachtsman in a boat less than 20 m long, you should keep out of the way of vessels in a narrow channel (Rule 9). In other words, you should not put yourself in a position where a close quarters situation might develop. This rule says that if, despite your best efforts, such a close-quarters situation does develop, you are still responsible for keeping out of his way no matter what aspect you are closing each other from.

And so does he (Rule 8(f)(iii)). In fact, there is no point in squabbling over who was in the right and who was in the wrong when you are both clutching to pieces of flotsam. Avoiding a collision is the responsibility of all concerned parties.

Rule 9. Narrow Channels

(a) A vessel proceeding along the course of a narrow channel or fairway shall keep as near to the outer limit of the channel or fairway which lies on her starboard side as is safe and practicable.

(b) A vessel of less than 20 meters in length or a sailing vessel shall not impede the passage of a vessel which can safely navigate only within a narrow channel or fairway.

[1]This is a good tip if you are worried about navigation too – if you can't see your entry marks for a harbour, or if you need more time to think through how you are going to carry off a berthing or anchoring evolution.

(c) A vessel engaged in fishing shall not impede the passage of any other vessel navigating within a narrow passage or fairway.

(d) A vessel shall not cross a narrow passage or fairway if such crossing impedes the passage of a vessel which can safely navigate only within such channel or fairway. The latter vessel may use the sound signal prescribed in Rule 34(d) if in doubt as to the intention of the crossing vessel.

(e)
  (i) In a narrow channel or fairway when overtaking can take place only when the vessel to be overtaken has to take action to permit safe passing, the vessel intending to overtake shall indicate her intention by sounding the appropriate signal prescribed in Rule 34(c)(i). The vessel to be overtaken shall, if in agreement, sound the appropriate signal prescribed in Rule 34(c)(ii) and take steps to permit safe passing. If in doubt she may sound the signals prescribed in Rule 34(d).
  (ii) This rule does not relieve the overtaking vessel of her obligation under Rule 13.

(f) A vessel nearing a bend or an area of a narrow channel or fairway where other vessels may be obscured by an intervening obstruction shall navigate with particular alertness and caution and shall sound the appropriate signal prescribed in Rule 34(e).

(g) Any vessel shall, if the circumstances of the case admit, avoid anchoring in a narrow channel.

This rule is discussed in more length in Section 4. This is the most sweeping departure from standard manoeuvring rules – for the simple reason that there is no alternative. If you are in a big ship in a small channel, you have no choice but to plough on. The rest of us must keep clear – there is no alternative. It is Rule of the Road by natural justice.

Rule 10. Traffic Separation Schemes

(a) This rule applies to traffic separation schemes adopted by the Organisation and does not relieve any vessel of her obligation under any other rule.

(b) A vessel using a traffic separation scheme shall:
  (i) Proceed in the appropriate traffic lane in the general direction of traffic flow for that lane.
  (ii) So far as is practicable keep clear of a traffic separation line or separation zone.
  (iii) Normally join or leave a traffic lane at the termination of the lane, but when joining or leaving from either side shall do so at as small an angle to the general direction of traffic flow as practicable.

(c) A vessel shall so far as practicable avoid crossing traffic lanes, but if obliged to do so shall cross on a heading as nearly as practicable at right angles to the general direction of traffic flow.

(d)

(i) A vessel shall not use an inshore traffic zone when she can safely use the appropriate traffic lane within the adjacent traffic separation scheme. However, vessels of less than 20 metres in length, sailing vessels and vessels engaged in fishing may use the inshore traffic zone.

(ii) Notwithstanding subparagraph (d)(i), a vessel may use an inshore traffic zone when en route to or from a port, offshore installation or structure, pilot station or any other place situated within the inshore traffic zone, or to avoid immediate danger.

(e) A vessel, other than a crossing vessel or a vessel joining or leaving a lane shall not normally enter a separation zone or cross a separation line except:

(i) In cases of emergency to avoid immediate danger;

(ii) To engage in fishing within a separation zone.

(f) A vessel navigating in areas near the terminations of traffic separation schemes shall do so with particular caution.

(g) A vessel shall so far as practicable avoid anchoring in a traffic separation scheme or in areas near its terminations.

(h) A vessel not using a traffic separation scheme shall avoid it by as wide a margin as is practicable.

(i) A vessel engaged in fishing shall not impede the passage of any vessel following a traffic lane.

(j) A vessel of less than 20 meters in length or a sailing vessel shall not impede the safe passage of a power driven vessel following a traffic lane.

(k) A vessel restricted in her ability to manoeuvre when engaged in an operation for the maintenance of safety of navigation in a traffic separating scheme is exempted from complying with this Rule to the extent necessary to carry out the operation.

(l) A vessel restricted in her ability to manoeuvre when engaged in an operation for the laying, servicing or picking up a submarine cable, within a traffic separating scheme, is exempted from complying with this Rule to the extent necessary to carry out the operation.

Again, the rules for separation schemes are fully discussed in Section 4. They are not so sweeping as those for narrow channels – and the reason behind this is that the channels are generally not so narrow: ships navigating in separation schemes do generally have manoeuvring options. But that apart, you should consider them to be maritime motorways, and pretty much react accordingly.

The big difference with the narrow channel rule (Rule 9) is that in a narrow channel, crossing vessels are not to impede a vessel that is restricted to a channel. Ships and boats longer than 20 metres crossing the

separation scheme are subject to standard 'crossing situation' rules (Rule 15). Vessels less than 20 metres in length – which includes the majority of us yachtsmen – should avoid impeding the passage of any vessel that is following the traffic lane.

From a yachtsman's perspective, I would say:
- *Whenever you can (which should be almost always), traverse the scheme in the inshore traffic zone.*
- *Only cross a separation scheme on a heading that is at right angles to the traffic flow in the scheme.*
- *Even then, try to cross when the traffic is relatively quiet. And …*
- *GO LIKE THE CLAPPERS.*

Section II - Conduct of Vessels in Sight of One Another

Rule 11. Application

Rules in this section apply to vessels in sight of one another.

Rule 12. Sailing Vessels

(a) When two sailing vessels are approaching one another, so as to involve risk of collision, one of them shall keep out of the way of the other as follows:

(i) When each of them has the wind on a different side, the vessel which has the wind on the port side shall keep out of the way of the other;

(ii) When both have the wind on the same side, the vessel which is to windward shall keep out of the way of the vessel which is to leeward;

(iii) If the vessel with the wind on the port side sees a vessel to windward and cannot determine with certainty whether the other vessel has the wind on the port or the starboard side, she shall keep out of the way of the other.

(b) For the purposes of this Rule the windward side shall be deemed to be the side opposite that on which the mainsail is carried or, in the case of a square rigged vessel, the side opposite to that on which the largest fore-and-aft sail is carried.

These are easy to remember
- *The starboard tack has right of way: starboard is a bigger word than port and can barge its way through.*
- *If both vessels are on the same tack, the one to windward has more freedom of manoeuvre and so should take the avoiding action.*

You are on the starboard tack when the wind is coming from your starboard side.

Rule 13. Overtaking

(a) Notwithstanding anything contained in the Rules of Part B, Sections I and II, any vessel overtaking any other shall keep out of the way of the vessel being overtaken.

(b) A vessel shall be deemed to be overtaking when coming up with a another vessel from a direction more than 22.5 degrees abaft her beam, that is, in such a position with reference to the vessel she is overtaking, that at night she would be able to see only the sternlight of that vessel but neither of her sidelights.

(c) When a vessel is in any doubt as to whether she is overtaking another, she shall assume that this is the case and act accordingly.

(d) Any subsequent alteration of the bearing between the two vessels shall not make the overtaking vessel a crossing vessel within the meaning of these Rules or relieve her of the duty of keeping clear of the overtaken vessel until she is finally past and clear.

There are 3 types of interaction between power driven vessels in sight of each other, that together comprise about 95% of all close-quarters interactions. These are:
- *Overtaking*
- *Head-on*
- *Crossing*

These are among the most important rules to have in your head. Each has its own rule: master these and you have pretty much cracked the Rule of the Road in sight of other vessels. The overtaking rule applies to all vessels in sight of each other, while the other two apply only to power driven vessels. They are all dealt with at some length in Section 4.

Rule 14. Head-on Situation

(a) When two power-driven vessels are meeting on reciprocal or nearly reciprocal courses so as to involve risk of collision each shall alter her course to starboard so that each shall pass on the port side of the other.

(b) Such a situation shall be deemed to exist when a vessel sees the other ahead or nearly ahead and by night she could see the masthead lights in line or nearly in line and/or both sidelights and by day she observes the corresponding aspect of the other vessel.

(c) When a vessel is in any doubt as to whether such a situation exists she shall assume that it does exist and act accordingly.

Don't try to be too fancy about defining when something is a head-on situation and when it is a crossing situation: one fades gently into the other. If you are at all concerned, go for it, and alter course to starboard!

Rule 15. Crossing Situation

When two power-driven vessels are crossing so as to involve risk of collision, the vessel which has the other on her own starboard side shall keep out of the way

and shall, if the circumstances of the case admit, avoid crossing ahead of the other vessel.

Rule 16. Action by Give-way Vessel

Every vessel which is directed to keep out of the way of another vessel shall, so far as possible, take early and substantial action to keep well clear.

Rule 17. Action by Stand-on Vessel

(a)
  (i) W here one of two vessels is to keep out of the way the other shall keep her course and speed.
  (ii) The latter vessel may however take action to avoid collision by her manoeuvre alone, as soon as it becomes apparent to her that the vessel required to keep out of the way is not taking appropriate action in accordance with these Rules.

(b) When, from any cause, the vessel required to keep her course and speed finds herself so close that collision cannot be avoided by the action of the give-way vessel alone, she shall take such action as will best aid to avoid collision.

(c) A power-driven vessel which takes action in a crossing situation in accordance with subparagraph (a)(ii) of this Rule to avoid collision with another power-driven vessel shall, if the circumstances of the case admit, not alter course to port for a vessel on her own port side.

(d) This Rule does not relieve the give-way vessel of her obligation to keep out of the way.

For the stand-on vessel, there are effectively 3 phases to a close-quarters situation:
Phase 1. Stand on and keep an eye on the other vessel. In 99% of cases, this is all that you need do.
Phase 2. As soon as it becomes clear that the give-way vessel is not taking appropriate action, and this decision needs to be made in the light of the prevailing circumstances, the stand-on vessel may take action to avoid a collision. When doing so, power driven vessels are encouraged not to alter course to port for a vessel on their own port side. (Doing so would put them directly in the path of the other vessel, should it at the last minute alter to starboard.... Draw it out: it sounds like double-dutch on paper, but makes sense as a diagram.)
Phase 3. When the stand-on vessel finds itself so close that, whatever happens, the give-way vessel would be unable to avoid a collision on her own, it may take any action to avoid a collision.

This explains why the term 'right of way' does not appear in the collision regulations. It is because the stand-on vessel, whilst encouraged initially to maintain course and speed (to make it easier for the give-way vessel to take effective action) nevertheless has a responsibility to take action if things start going wrong. Ultimately, no one can claim to have right of way.

Rule 18. Responsibilities Between Vessels

Except where rule 9, 10, and 13 otherwise require:
(a) A power driven vessel underway shall keep out of the way of:
   (i) A vessel not under command;
   (ii) A vessel restricted in her ability to manoeuvre;
   (iii) A vessel engaged in fishing;
   (iv) A sailing vessel;

(b) A sailing vessel under way shall keep out of the way of:
   (i) A vessel not under command;
   (ii) A vessel restricted in her ability to manoeuvre;
   (iii) A vessel engaged in fishing;

(c) A vessel engaged in fishing when underway shall, so far as possible, keep out of the way of:
   (i) A vessel not under command;
   (ii) A vessel restricted in her ability to manoeuvre.

(d)
   (i) Any vessel other than a vessel not under command or a vessel restricted in her ability to manoeuvre shall, if the circumstances of the case admit, avoid impeding the safe passage of a vessel constrained by her draft, exhibiting the signals in Rule 28.
   (ii) A vessel constrained by her draft shall navigate with particular caution having full regard to her special condition.

(e) A seaplane on the water shall, in general, keep well clear of all vessels and avoid impeding their navigation. In circumstances, however, where risk of collision exists, she shall comply with the Rules of this Part.

This is the 'hierarchy rule' explained in more detail in Section 4. It does not supersede the Rules for narrow channels, separation schemes or overtaking vessels. To a yachtsman, it is saying 'do what you possibly can through early manoeuvring so that you don't even consider a close quarters situation with less manoeuvrable vessels. If you do find yourself close to them, make sure that you keep clear.'

It is not an open invitation for sailors to zoom in front of supertankers bleating 'steam gives way to sail' on VHF. *Where possible they will alter to avoid you (or at least the more professional ones will), but they are not easy to manoeuvre, and it is very much more sensible for you to do everything possible to avoid them.*

Section III - Conduct of Vessels in Restricted Visibility

Rule 19. Conduct of Vessels in Restricted Visibility

(a) This Rule applies to vessels not in sight of one another when navigating in or near an area of restricted visibility.

(b) Every vessel shall proceed at a safe speed adapted to the prevailing circumstances and condition of restricted visibility. A power-driven vessel shall have her engines ready for immediate manoeuvre.

(c) Every vessel shall have due regard to the prevailing circumstances and conditions of restricted visibility when complying with the Rules of Section I of this Part.

(d) A vessel which detects by radar alone the presence of another vessel shall determine if a close-quarters situation is developing and/or risk of collision exists. If so, she shall take avoiding action in ample time, provided that when such action consists of an alteration in course, so far as possible the following shall be avoided:
   (i) An alteration of course to port for a vessel forward of the beam, other than for a vessel being overtaken;
   (ii) An alteration of course toward a vessel abeam or abaft the beam.

(e) Except where it has been determined that a risk of collision does not exist, every vessel which hears apparently forward of her beam the fog signal of another vessel, or which cannot avoid a close-quarters situation with another vessel forward of her beam, shall reduce her speed to be the minimum at which she can be kept on her course. She shall if necessary take all her way off and in any event navigate with extreme caution until danger of collision is over.

Look at Rule 19a. '...vessels not in sight of each other ... when navigating in or near an area of restricted visibility.' These rules apply even if you are in clear visibility, but steaming close to a fog bank where you might not be able to see the other vessel. I have very often seen fog banks rolling in across the English Channel that are so clear-cut they could almost be a curtain. 180 degrees of horizon are sparkling clear and the rest is grey damp fog. In one direction you are working to one set of Rules, and elsewhere you are working to the other.

Rule 19b. I would not want to teach my granny to suck eggs, but speaking entirely personally, when I and my sailing boat are in or close to restricted visibility I always start my engine and either motor or motor sail. Without foresails, the all-round visibility is improved and, while the engine might be noisy, it makes the boat very much more responsive in a crisis.

Rules 19d and e refer to two different sets of action that apply in restricted visibility. If you can pick up a vessel on radar in good time, you should alter course to avoid a close quarters situation. If however you get close enough to another vessel to hear a fog signal, you should proceed with caution. You cannot always guarantee that the fog signal you hear correlates to a contact on radar, or that you have picked up all contacts within the ground clutter, particularly in rough conditions.

Part C - Lights and Shapes

All these rules are important and yachtsmen need to be at least familiar with the general principles. Rather than plough through the rules, I suggest that you turn to Section 2, where they are discussed in some detail. For that reason, I have not put much interpretation against these Rules.

Come back to this bit if you are a genuine glutton for punishment!

Rule 20. Application

(a) Rules in this part shall be complied with in all weathers.

(b) The Rules concerning lights shall be complied with from sunset to sunrise, and during such times no other lights shall be exhibited, except such lights which cannot be mistaken for the lights specified in these Rules or do not impair their visibility or distinctive character, or interfere with the keeping of a proper look-out.

(c) The lights prescribed by these rules shall, if carried, also be exhibited from sunrise to sunset in restricted visibility and may be exhibited in all other circumstances when it is deemed necessary. *Don't hesitate: if you think that navigation lights would help you to be seen – put them on!*

(d) The Rules concerning shapes shall be complied with by day.

(e) The lights and shapes specified in these Rules shall comply with the provisions of Annex I to these Regulations.

Rule 21. Definitions

(a) 'Masthead light' means a white light placed over the fore and aft centreline of the vessel showing an unbroken light over an arc of horizon of 225 degrees and so fixed as to show the light from right ahead to 22.5 degrees abaft the beam on either side of the vessel.

(b) 'Sidelights' means a green light on the starboard side and a red light on the port side each showing an unbroken light over an arc of horizon of 112.5 degrees and so fixed as to show the light from right ahead to 22.5 degrees abaft the beam on the respective side. In a vessel of less than 20 metres in length the sidelights may be combined in one lantern carried on the fore and aft centreline of the vessel.

(c) 'Sternlight', means a white light placed as nearly as practicable at the stern showing an unbroken light over an arc of horizon of 135 degrees and so fixed as to show the light 67.5 degrees from right aft on each side of the vessel.

(d) 'Towing light' means a yellow light having the same characteristics as the 'sternlight' defined in paragraph (c) of this Rule.

e) 'All round light' means a light showing an unbroken light over an arc of horizon of 360 degrees.

(f) Flashing light' means a light flashing at regular intervals at a frequency of 120 flashes or more per minute.

Rule 22. Visibility of Lights

The lights prescribed in these Rules shall have an intensity as specified in Section 8 of Annex I to these Regulations so as to be visible at the following minimum ranges:

(a) In vessels of 50 meters or more in length:
- a masthead light, 6 miles;
- a sidelight, 3 miles;
- a towing light, 3 miles;
- a white red, green or yellow all-around light, 3 miles.

(b) In vessels of 12 meters or more in length but less than 50 meters in length:
- a masthead light, 5 miles; except that where the length of the vessel is less than 20 meters, 3 miles;
- a sidelight, 2 miles;
- a sternlight, 2 miles,
- a towing light, 2 miles;
- a white, red, green or yellow all-round light, 2 miles.

(c) In vessels of less than 12 meters in length:
- a masthead light, 2 miles;
- a sidelight, 1 mile;
- a towing light, 2 miles;
- a white red, green or yellow all-around light, 2 miles.

(d) In inconspicuous, partly submerged vessels or objects being towed:
- a white all-round light, 3 miles.

Rule 23. Power-driven Vessels Underway

(a) A power-driven vessel underway shall exhibit:
  (i) A masthead light forward;
  (ii) A second masthead light abaft of and higher than the forward one; except that a vessel of less than 50 metres in length shall not be obliged to exhibit such a light, but may do so.
  (iii) Sidelights; and
  (iv) A sternlight.

(b) An air-cushion vessel when operating in non-displacement mode shall, in addition to the lights prescribed in paragraph (a) of this Rule, exhibit an all-round flashing yellow light.

(c)
    (i) A power-driven vessel of less than 12 metres in length may in lieu of the lights prescribed in paragraph (a) of this Rule exhibit an all-round white light and sidelights.

    (ii) A power-driven vessel of less than 7 metres in length whose maximum speed does not exceed 7 knots may in lieu of the lights prescribed in paragraph (a) of this Rule exhibit an all-round white light and shall, if practicable, also exhibit sidelights.

    (iii) The masthead light or all-round white light on a power-driven vessel of less than 12 metres in length may be displaced from the fore and aft centreline of the vessel if centreline fitting is not practicable, provided the sidelights are combined in one lantern which shall be carried on the fore and aft centreline of the vessel or located as nearly as practicable in the same fore and aft line as the masthead light or all-round white light.

Rule 24. Towing and Pushing

(a) A power driven vessel when towing shall exhibit:
    (i) Instead of the light prescribed in Rule 23(a)(i) or (a)(ii), two masthead lights in a vertical line. When the length of the tow measuring from the stern of the towing vessel to the after end of the tow exceeds 200 meters, three such lights in a vertical line;
    (ii) Sidelights;
    (iii) A sternlight;
    (iv) A towing light in a vertical line above the sternlight;
and
    (v) When the length of the tow exceeds 200 meters, a diamond shape where it can best be seen.

(b) When a pushing vessel and a vessel being pushed ahead are rigidly connected in a composite unit they shall be regarded as a power-driven vessel and exhibit the lights prescribed in Rule 23.

(c) A power-driven vessel when pushing ahead or towing alongside, except in the case of a composite unit, shall exhibit:
    (i) Instead of the light prescribed in Rule 23(a)(i) or (a)(ii), two masthead lights in a vertical line. When the length of the tow measuring from the stern of the towing vessel to the after end of the tow exceeds 200 metres, three such lights in a vertical line;
    (ii) Sidelights;
    (iii) A sternlight.

(d) A power-driven vessel to which paragraph (a) or (c) of this Rule apply shall also comply with Rule 23(a)(ii).

Rule 23(a)(ii) says that a power driven vessel longer than 50 metres must, and a power driven vessel of less than 50 metres may, carry a second steaming light abaft and above the forward one. This also applies when towing.

(e) A vessel or object being towed, other than those mentioned in paragraph (g) of this Rule, shall exhibit:
    (i) Sidelights;
    (ii) A sternlight;
    (iii) When the length of the tow exceeds 200 metres, a diamond shape where it can best be seen.

(f) Provided that any number of vessels being towed alongside or pushed in a group shall be lighted as one vessel,
    (i) a vessel being pushed ahead, not being part of a composite unit, shall exhibit at the forward end, sidelights;
    (ii) a vessel being towed alongside shall exhibit a sternlight and at the forward end, sidelights.

(g) An inconspicuous, partly submerged vessel or object, or combination of such vessels or objects being towed, shall exhibit:
    (i) If it is less than 25 metres in breadth, one all-round white light at or near the front end and one at or near the after end except that dracones need not exhibit a light at or near the forward end;
    (ii) If it is 25 metres or more in breadth, two or more additional all-round white lights at or near the extremities of its breadth;
    (iii) If it exceeds 100 metres in length, additional all-round white lights between the lights prescribed in subparagraphs (i) and (ii) so that the distance between the lights shall not exceed 100 meters;
    (iv) A diamond shape at or near the aftermost extremity of the last vessel or object being towed and if the length of the tow exceeds 200 meters an additional diamond shape where it can best be seen and located as far forward as is practicable.

(h) When from any sufficient cause it is impracticable for a vessel or object being towed to exhibit the lights or shapes prescribed in paragraph (e) or (g) of this Rule, all possible measures shall be taken to light the vessel or object being towed or at least indicate the presence of such vessel or object.
    (i) Where from any sufficient cause it is impracticable for a vessel not normally engaged in towing operations to display the lights prescribed in paragraph (a) or (c) of this Rule, such vessel shall not be required to exhibit those lights when engaged in towing another vessel in distress or otherwise in need of assistance. All possible measures shall be taken to indicate the nature of the relationship between the towing vessel and the vessel being towed as authorised by Rule 36, in particular by illuminating the towline.

Rule 36 authorises you to attract attention by any light signal that may not be mistaken for a navigation light – except for a strobe light. The most normal way of doing this (and the only one that I have ever seen a yacht use) is with a searchlight or a torch. If you are going to do this, shine it at the water in the general direction of another vessel, not directly at anybody. You can destroy someone's night vision in a flash (literally!).

Rule 24(i) is important for yachtsman. You take someone in tow and suddenly it gets dark: how are you going to prevent another boat from trying to cross the towline? You are allowed to use your own navigation lights instead of towing lights, but this just increases the confusion of the other guy. You must do everything you can to let people know that a tow is taking place. If you can do so, get a floodlight rigged so that if anyone approaches you can shine a light direct on the towline.

Now have a look at it from the other vessel. You are gently sailing or motoring through the night, your mind a blank with the exception of two active grey cells that are counting down the seconds until you are reunited with your sleeping bag. You see a couple of small boats motoring along in close proximity to each other. One is lit normally, and you can't see a masthead steaming light on the other. There is a searchlight playing on the surface of the water between the two of them. Would you know what to make of it?

I guarantee that 99% of us would think that they are just messing about.... There is no harm in just lodging this in the back of your mind so that if you ever DO see this, you know what it is.

Rule 25. Sailing Vessels Underway and Vessels Under Oars

(a) A sailing vessel underway shall exhibit:
  (i) Sidelights;
  (ii) A sternlight.

(b) In a sailing vessel of less than 20 meters in length the lights prescribed in paragraph (a) of this Rule may be combined in one lantern carried at or near the top of the mast where it can best be seen.

(c) A sailing vessel underway may, in addition to the lights prescribed in paragraph (a) of this Rule, exhibit at or near the top of the mast, where they can best be seen, two all-round lights in a vertical line, the upper being red and the lower green, but these lights shall not be exhibited in conjunction with the combined lantern permitted by paragraph (b) of this Rule.

(d)
  (i) A sailing vessel of less than 7 meters in length shall, if practicable, exhibit the lights prescribed in paragraph (a) or (b) of this Rule, but if she does not, she shall have ready at hand an electric torch or lighted lantern showing a white light which shall be exhibited in sufficient time to prevent collision.
  (ii) A vessel under oars may exhibit the lights prescribed in this rule for sailing vessels, but if she does not, she shall have ready at hand an electric torch or lighted lantern showing a white light which shall be exhibited in sufficient time to prevent collision.

(e) A vessel proceeding under sail when also being propelled by machinery shall exhibit forward where it can best be seen a conical shape, apex downwards.

Rule 26. Fishing Vessels

(a) A vessel engaged in fishing, whether underway or at anchor, shall exhibit only the lights and shapes prescribed by this rule.

(b) A vessel when engaged in trawling, by which is meant the dragging through the water of a dredge net or other apparatus used as a fishing appliance, shall exhibit:
  (i) Two all-round lights in a vertical line, the upper being green and the lower white, or a shape consisting of two cones with their apexes together in a vertical line one above the other; a vessel of less than 20 meters in length may instead of this shape exhibit a basket;
  (ii) A masthead light abaft of and higher than the all-round green light; a vessel of less than 50 meters in length shall not be obliged to exhibit such a light but may do so;
  (iii) When making way through the water, in addition to the lights prescribed in this paragraph, sidelights and a sternlight.

(c) A vessel engaged in fishing, other than trawling, shall exhibit:
  (i) Two all-round lights in a vertical line, the upper being red and the lower white, or a shape consisting of two cones with their apexes together in a vertical line one above the other; a vessel of less than 20 meters in length may instead of this shape exhibit a basket;
  (ii) When there is outlying gear extending more than 150 metres horizontally from the vessel, an all-round white light or a cone apex upwards in the direction of the gear.
  (iii) When making way through the water, in addition to the lights prescribed in this paragraph, sidelights and a sternlight.

(d) A vessel engaged in fishing in close proximity to other vessels engaged in fishing may exhibit the additional signals described in Annex II to these Regulations.

Annex II is all about how fishing vessels, working in close proximity, signal their actions in order to allow other vessels to keep out of their way. In a lifetime working at sea, I have occasionally (and very unwillingly) found myself surrounded by too many fishing vessels for comfort, but I have never seen these signals being used in anger. The rules are worth a read: you never know when you might come across them, but my advice is to give them a quick cursory skim and then store them away in the deeper recesses of your mind.

A more valuable tip for yachtsmen is, wherever possible, to avoid concentrations of fishermen. Except in the pub where, in my experience, they can be excellent company. I was once invited to a stag night in Polperro...

(e) A vessel when not engaged in fishing shall not exhibit the lights or shapes prescribed in this Rule, but only those prescribed for a vessel of her length.

Dream on!

I am sure that there are fishing vessels that religiously switch off their lights or take down their shapes when not engaged in fishing. But you could almost certainly count their numbers on the fingers of one hand. In fact, it is quite instructive to take time out and have a quick wander round a fishing port: at a rough guess 100% of all fishing boats that you see will have their shapes still in place in the rigging. About 10% will be showing their navigation and fishing lights even though they are safely tucked up alongside. Personally, I don't take great issue with this. These men and women have a tough life at sea and I admire them hugely for it. I am quite prepared to give them priority, irrespective of whether they are fishing or on passage.

Rule 27. Vessels Not Under Command or Restricted in Their Ability to Manoeuvre

(a) A vessel not under command shall exhibit:
  (i) Two all-round red lights in a vertical line where they can best be seen;
  (ii) Two balls or similar shapes in a vertical line where they can best be seen;
  (iii) When making way through the water, in addition to the lights prescribed in this paragraph, sidelights and a sternlight.

The definition of a vessel not under command is set out in Rule 3f. It includes all types of vessel that, because of some unusual circumstance, are unable to fulfil their obligations for collision avoidance. In practice, machinery breakdown and steering gear failure are likely to be the most common causes, although there are undoubtedly others.

It goes without saying that this category only applies to vessels that are under way. By definition, if you drop the anchor (and it holds) you have once more taken command of the ship.

(b) A vessel restricted in her ability to manoeuvre, except a vessel engaged in mineclearance operations, shall exhibit:
  (i) Three all-round lights in a vertical line where they can best be seen. The highest and lowest of these lights shall be red and the middle light shall be white;
  (ii) Three shapes in a vertical line where they can best be seen. The highest and lowest of these shapes shall be balls and the middle one a diamond.
  (iii) When making way through the water, a masthead light, sidelights and a sternlight in addition to the lights prescribed in subparagraph (i);
  (iv) When at anchor, in addition to the lights or shapes prescribed in subparagraphs(i) and (ii), the light, lights, or shape prescribed in Rule 30.

The definition of a vessel restricted in its ability to manoeuvre is set out in Rule 3g. These vessels are in some way hampered in their ability to respond as expected to a close quarters situation by the nature of their employment. Some of the more likely causes are also set out in the rule, but there is nothing to prevent a skipper from declaring himself RAM in circumstances that are not formally foreseen in these rules.

This rule can apply to vessels that are not under way, specifically when conducting diving operations at anchor, or laying navigation marks. It then becomes a signal to other vessels to keep clear.

(c) A power-driven vessel engaged in a towing operation such as severely restricts the towing vessel and her tow in their ability to deviate from their course shall, in addition to the lights or shapes prescribed in Rule 24(a), exhibit the lights or shapes prescribed in subparagraph (b)(i) and (ii) of this Rule.

(d) A vessel engaged in dredging or underwater operations, when restricted in her ability to manoeuvre, shall exhibit the lights and shapes prescribed in subparagraphs (b)(i),(ii) and (iii) of this Rule and shall in addition when an obstruction exists, exhibit:
  (i) Two all-round red lights or two balls in a vertical line to indicate the side on which the obstruction exists;
  (ii) Two all-round green lights or two diamonds in a vertical line to indicate the side on which another vessel may pass;
  (iii) When at anchor, the lights or shapes prescribed in this paragraph instead of the lights or shapes prescribed in Rule 30.

(e) Whenever the size of a vessel engaged in diving operations makes it impracticable to exhibit all lights and shapes prescribed in paragraph (d) of this Rule, the following shall be exhibited:
  (i) Three all-round lights in a vertical line where they can best be seen. The highest and lowest of these lights shall be red and the middle light shall be white;
  (ii) A rigid replica of the code flag 'A' not less than 1 meter in height. Measures shall be taken to ensure its all-round visibility.

(f) A vessel engaged in mineclearance operations shall in addition to the lights prescribed for a power-driven vessel in Rule 23 or to the light or shape prescribed for a vessel at anchor in Rule 30 as appropriate, exhibit three all-round green lights or three balls. One of these lights or shapes shall be exhibited near the foremast head and one at each end of the fore yard. These lights or shapes indicate that it is dangerous for another vessel to approach within 1000 meters of the mineclearance vessel.

(g) Vessels of less than 12 meters in length, except those engaged in diving operations, shall not be required to exhibit the lights prescribed in this Rule.

(h) The signals prescribed in this Rule are not signals

of vessels in distress and requiring assistance. Such signals are contained in Annex IV to these Regulations.

This last section is important. If a vessel wants your assistance, it will become quite obvious, either through an emergency signal, or quite simply by him calling you up on VHF. I have been through all kinds of exciting and debilitating evolutions on the bridge of various of Her Majesty's Warships. Believe me, the last thing you need when you are up to your elbows in alligators is to be polite to a well-meaning, if misguided, yachtsman offering you a cup of tea and a sweet biscuit.

Rule 28. Vessels Constrained by their Draft

A vessel constrained by her draft may, in addition to the lights prescribed for power-driven vessels in Rule 23, exhibit where they can best be seen three all-round red lights in a vertical line, or a cylinder.

Note the deliberate use of the word 'may' here.

Big ships do not have to show the lights and shapes for a vessel constrained by its draught. If it came to a legal judgment, they would have no grounds for claiming priority if the shapes and lights had not been shown, but that won't be much consolation to you sitting in the wheelhouse dodging 100,000 tons of steel that is trying to play tag with you. My advice would be to stay well clear of anything that looks big and appears to be navigating in enclosed waters. (Besides which, it is not always easy to see shapes on a big ship, and it may not be until it is passing that they become visible.)

Rule 29. Pilot Vessels

(a) A vessel engaged on pilotage duty shall exhibit:
  (i) At or near the masthead, two all-round lights in a vertical line, the upper being white and the lower red;
  (ii) When underway, in addition, sidelights and a sternlight;
  (iii) When at anchor, in addition to the lights prescribed in subparagraph (i), the lights or shape prescribed in Rule 30 for vessels at anchor.

(b) A pilot vessel when not engaged on pilotage duty shall exhibit the lights or shapes prescribed for a similar vessel of her length.

Rule 30. Anchored Vessels and Vessels Aground

(a) A vessel at anchor shall exhibit where it can best be seen:
  (i) In the fore part, an all-round white light or one ball;
  (ii) At or near the stern and at a lower level than the light prescribed in subparagraph (i), an all-round white light.

(b) A vessel of less than 50 meters in length may exhibit an all-round white light where it can best be seen instead of the lights prescribed in paragraph (a) of this Rule.

(c) A vessel at anchor may, and a vessel of 100 meters and more in length shall, also use the available working or equivalent lights to illuminate her decks.

(d) A vessel aground shall exhibit the lights prescribed in paragraph (a) or (b) of this Rule and in addition, where they can best be seen;
  (i) Two all-round red lights in a vertical line;
  (ii) Three balls in a vertical line.

(e) A vessel of less than 7 meters in length, when at anchor not in or near a narrow channel, fairway or where other vessels normally navigate, shall not be required to exhibit the shape prescribed in paragraphs (a) and (b) of this Rule.

(f) A vessel of less than 12 meters in length, when aground, shall not be required to exhibit the lights or shapes prescribed in subparagraphs (d)(i) and (ii) of this Rule.

Sneaky question to ask your Yachtmaster instructor:
* *Is a vessel whose anchor is dragging considered to be at anchor or under way?*

The answer is that you cannot be considered to be at anchor unless your anchor is fast on the bottom; a dragging anchor therefore means that you are, by the strictest interpretation of the rules, under way.

Rule 31. Seaplanes

Where it is impracticable for a seaplane to exhibit lights or shapes of the characteristics or in the positions prescribed in the Rules of this Part she shall exhibit lights and shapes as closely similar in characteristics and position as is possible.

In the event, the rules of the air and those of the sea mean that a seaplane's flying lights are very similar to those required on the water, although the spacing between lights may appear a little strange.

Part D - Sound and Light Signals

Rule 32. Definitions

(a) The word 'whistle' means any sound signalling appliance capable of producing the prescribed blasts and which complies with the specifications in Annex III to these Regulations.

(b) The term 'short blast' means a blast of about one second's duration.

(c) The term 'prolonged blast' means a blast from four to six seconds' duration.

You are a better person than me if you can make head or tail of Annex III to the Rules – but don't let me stop you from having a crack at it.

Rule 33. Equipment for Sound Signals

(a) A vessel of 12 metres or more in length shall be provided with a whistle and a bell and a vessel of 100 metres or more in length shall, in addition be provided with a gong, the tone and sound of which cannot be confused with that of the bell. The whistle, bell and gong shall comply with the specifications in Annex III to these Regulations. The bell or gong or both may be replaced by other equipment having the same respective sound characteristics, provided that manual sounding of the prescribed signals shall always be possible.

(b) A vessel of less than 12 metres in length shall not be obliged to carry the sound signalling appliances prescribed in paragraph (a) of this Rule but if she does not, she shall be provided with some other means of making an efficient signal.

From the point of view of sound signaling apparatus, there are 3 distinct length bands:
- ***Vessels less than 12 metres in length.*** *No need for whistles, gongs or bells, but must have something to advertise its presence in an efficient manner – normally a small aerosol foghorn bought from the marina chandlery.*
- ***Vessels greater than 12 metres in length,*** *but less than 100 metres. A whistle and a bell. The whistle for when it is making way, and the bell for when it is at anchor or aground.*
- ***A vessel greater than 100 metres in length.*** *A whistle for when it is making way. A bell (forward) and a gong (aft) for when it is at anchor or aground.*

Rule 34. Manoeuvring and Warning Signals

(a) When vessels are in sight of one another, a power-driven vessel under way, when manoeuvring as authorised or required by these Rules, shall indicate that manoeuvre by the following signals on her whistle:

- one short blast to mean 'I am altering my course to starboard';
- two short blasts to mean 'I am altering my course to port';
- three short blasts to mean 'I am operating astern propulsion'.

(b) Any vessel may supplement the whistle signals prescribed in paragraph (a) of this Rule by light signals, repeated as appropriate, whilst the manoeuvre is being carried out.
   (i)   These signals shall have the following significance:
   - one flash to mean 'I am altering my course to starboard';
   - two flashes to mean 'I am altering my course to port';
   - three flashes to mean 'I am operating astern propulsion'.
   (ii) The duration of each flash shall be about one second, the interval between flashes shall be about one second, and the interval between successive signals shall not be less than ten seconds.
   (iii) The light used for this signal shall, if fitted, be an all-round white light, visible at a minimum range of 5 miles, and shall comply with the provisions of Annex I to these Regulations.

There is a fast ball for the unwary here.

*Note that the manoeuvring **sound** signals are proscribed for power driven vessels only and that manoeuvring **light** signals may be used by all vessels (including sailing vessels). That's not to say that sailing vessels can't make a manoeuvring sound signal, although I for one have never heard one do so. Sailing vessels can, of course make other sound signals: they certainly do in fog, and Rule 34d stipulates that they should make 5 short blasts when in sight of another vessel and uncertain about its intentions. Don't ask me why this is. It is like gravity, or the direction that water circulates when you take out the plug in your bath – just one of those things*

*You also should note that **manoeuvring sound signals are mandatory** for power driven vessels when manoeuvring as required by the rules (in other words when taking appropriate action to avoid a collision). Supplementing them with a **manoeuvring light signal, however, is optional.***

(c) When in sight of one another in a narrow channel or fairway:
   (i)   A vessel intending to overtake another shall in compliance with Rule 9 (e)(i) indicate her intention by the following signals on her whistle.
   - Two prolonged blasts followed by one short blast to mean 'I intend to overtake you on your starboard side';
   - Two prolonged blasts followed by two short blasts to mean 'I intend to overtake you on your port side'.
   (ii) The vessel about to be overtaken when acting

in accordance with 9(e)(i) shall indicate her agreement by the following signal on her whistle:

- one prolonged, one short, one prolonged and one short blast, in that order.

If the vessel to be overtaken doesn't like the idea, Rule 9e authorises it to give 5 short blasts to show that it is in doubt.

(d) When vessels in sight of one another are approaching each other and from any cause either vessel fails to understand the intentions or actions of the other, or is in doubt whether sufficient action is being taken by the other to avoid collision, the vessel in doubt shall immediately indicate such doubt by giving at least five short and rapid blasts on the whistle. Such signal may be supplemented by at least five short and rapid flashes.

(e) A vessel nearing a bend or an area of a channel or fairway where other vessels may be obscured by an intervening obstruction shall sound one prolonged blast. Such signal shall be answered with a prolonged blast by any approaching vessel that may be within hearing around the bend or behind the intervening obstruction.

(f) If whistles are fitted on a vessel at a distance apart of more than 100 meters, one whistle only shall be used for giving manoeuvring and warning signals.

With the exception of Rule 34e, these are all sound signals for vessels that are in sight of each other. When they cannot see each other due to restricted visibility, Rule 35 applies and Rule 34 is not used.

Rule 35. Sound Signals in Restricted Visibility

In or near an area of restricted visibility, whether by day or night the signals prescribed in this Rule shall be used as follows:

(a) A power-driven vessel making way through the water shall sound at intervals of not more than 2 minutes one prolonged blast.

(b) A power-driven vessel underway but stopped and making no way through the water shall sound at intervals of no more than 2 minutes two prolonged blasts in succession with an interval of about 2 seconds between them.

(c) A vessel not under command, a vessel restricted in her ability to manoeuvre, a vessel constrained by her draft, a sailing vessel, a vessel engaged in fishing and a vessel engaged in towing or pushing another vessel shall, instead of the signals prescribed in paragraph (a) or (b) of this Rule, sound at intervals of not more than 2 minutes three blasts in succession, namely one prolonged followed by two short blasts.

(d) A vessel engaged in fishing, when at anchor, and a vessel restricted in her ability to manoeuvre when carrying out her work at anchor, shall instead of the signals prescribed in paragraph (g) of this Rule sound the signal prescribed in paragraph (c) of this Rule.

(e) A vessel towed or if more than one vessel is being towed the last vessel of the tow, if manned, shall at intervals of not more than 2 minutes sound four blasts in succession, namely one prolonged followed by three short blasts. When practicable, this signal shall be made immediately after the signal made by the towing vessel.

(f) When a pushing vessel and a vessel being pushed ahead are rigidly connected in a composite unit they shall be regarded as a power-driven vessel and shall give the signals prescribed in paragraphs (a) or (b) of this Rule.

(g) A vessel at anchor shall at intervals of not more than 1 minute ring the bell rapidly for five seconds. In a vessel 100 meters or more in length the bell shall be sounded in the forepart of the vessel and immediately after the ringing of the bell the gong shall be sounded rapidly for about 5 seconds in the after part of the vessel. A vessel at anchor may in addition sound three blasts in succession, namely one short, one long and one short blast, to give warning of her position and of the possibility of collision to an approaching vessel.

(h) A vessel aground shall give the bell signal and if required the gong signal prescribed in paragraph (g) of this Rule and shall, in addition, give three separate and distinct strokes on the bell immediately before and after the rapid ringing of the bell. A vessel aground may in addition sound an appropriate whistle signal.

(i) A vessel of less than 12 meters in length shall not be obliged to give the above mentioned signals but, if she does not, shall make some other efficient sound signal at intervals of not more than 2 minutes.

(j) A pilotage vessel when engaged on pilotage duty may in addition to the signals prescribed in paragraph (a), (b) or (g) of this Rule sound an identity signal consisting of four short blasts.

Rule 36. Signals to Attract Attention

If necessary to attract the attention of another vessel, any vessel may make light or sound signals that cannot be mistaken for any signal authorised elsewhere in these Rules, or may direct the beam of her searchlight in the direction of the danger, in such a way as not to embarrass any vessel. Any light to attract the attention of another vessel shall be such that it cannot be mistaken for any aid to navigation. For the purpose of this Rule the use of high intensity intermittent or revolving lights, such as strobe lights, shall be avoided.

It takes 20 minutes to get effective night vision and a thoughtless sweep of a searchlight to destroy it. Never point a light at the bridge or steering position of another vessel.

Sailing boats often illuminate their sails when they want to draw attention to themselves; it would certainly help, but I am never too certain how effective this really is when you are standing 100 feet out of the water on the bridge of a large merchant ship. It is probably more effective to provide some sort of flash in the general direction of an approaching vessel (although not at the bridge) which may well get more attention.

Rule 37. Distress Signals

When a vessel is in distress and requires assistance she shall use or exhibit the signals described in Annex IV to these Regulations.

Worth knowing. See Section 7.

Part E - Exemptions

Rule 38. Exemptions

Any vessel (or class of vessel) provided that she complies with the requirements of the International Regulations for the Preventing of Collisions at Sea, 1960, the keel of which is laid or is at a corresponding stage of construction before the entry into force of these Regulations may be exempted from compliance therewith as follows:

(a) The installation of lights with ranges prescribed in Rule 22, until 4 years after the date of entry into force of these regulations.
(b) The installation of lights with colour specifications as prescribed in Section 7 of Annex I to these Regultions, until 4 years after the entry into force of these Regulations.

(c) The repositioning of lights as a result of conversion from Imperial to metric units and rounding off measurement figures, permanent exemption.

(d)
   (i) The repositioning of masthead lights on vessels of less than 150 meters in length, resulting from the prescriptions of Section 3 (a) of Annex I to these regulations, permanent exemption.
   (ii) The repositioning of masthead lights on vessels of 150 meters or more in length, resulting from the prescriptions of Section 3 (a) of Annex I to these regulations, until 9 years after the date of entry into force of these Regulations.

(e) The repositioning of masthead lights resulting from the prescriptions of Section 2(b) of Annex I to these Regulations, until 9 years after the date of entry into force of these Regulations.

(f) The repositioning of sidelights resulting from the prescriptions of Section 2(g) and 3(b) of Annex I to these Regulations, until 9 years after the date of entry into force of these Regulations.

(g) The requirements for sound signal appliances prescribed in Annex II to these Regulations, until 9 years after the date of entry into force of these Regulations.

(h) The repositioning of all-round lights resulting from the prescription of Section 9(b) of Annex I to these Regulations, permanent exemption.

These are not significant, and inserted for the sake of completeness only.

Annex I
Positioning and technical details of lights and shapes

By now, you have earned a bit of a break. This section is technical and of little relevance to the yachtsman. I have included it on the grounds that one reader in 10,000 (I wish) may be interested in the sort of detail that it contains. For the first 9,999 of you, however, I should make a cup of tea and take this opportunity to put your feet up.

For interest and before we start, it is worth having a look at Annex II, and making yourself quite familiar with Annex IV (Emergency signals). I am prepared to let you off Annex III.

1. Definition.

The term 'height above the hull' means height above the uppermost continuous deck. This height shall be measured from the position vertically beneath the location of the light.

2. Vertical positioning and spacing of lights.

(a) On a power driven vessel of 20 metres or more in length the masthead lights shall be placed as follows:

(i) The forward masthead light, or if only one masthead light is carried, then that light, at a height above the hull of not less than 6 metres, and, if the breadth of the vessel exceeds 6 metres, then at a height above the hull not less than such breadth, so however that the light need not be placed at a greater height above the hull than 12 metres.
(ii) When 2 masthead lights are carried the after one shall be at least 4.5 metres vertically higher than the forward one.

(b) The vertical separation of masthead lights of power driven vessels shall be such that in all normal conditions of trim the after light will be seen over and separate from the forward light at a distance of 1,000 metres from the stem when viewed at sea level.

(c) The masthead light of a power driven vessel of 12 metres but less than 20 metres in length shall be placed at a height above the gunwale of not less than 2.5 metres.

(d) A power driven vessel of less than 12 metres in length may carry the uppermost light at a height of less than 2.5 metres above the gunwale. When however a masthead light is carried in addition to sidelights and a sternlight or the all-round light proscribed in Rule 23(c)(i) is carried in addition to sidelights, then such masthead light or all-round light shall be carried at least 1 metre higher than the sidelights.

(e) One of the two or three masthead lights prescribed for a power driven vessel when engaged in towing or pushing another vessel shall be placed in the same position as either the forward masthead light or the after masthead light; provided that, if carried on the aftermast, the lowest after masthead light shall be at least 4.5 metres vertically higher than the forward masthead light.

(f)

(i) The masthead light or lights prescribed in Rule 23(a) shall be so placed as to be above and clear of all other lights and obstructions except as described in sub-paragraph (ii).
(ii) When it is impractical to carry the all-round lights prescribed by Rule 27(b)(i) or Rule 28 below the masthead lights, they may be carried above the after masthead light(s) or vertically in between the forward masthead light(s) and after masthead light(s), provided that in the latter case the requirement of Section 3(c) of this Annex shall be complied with.

(g) The sidelights of a power driven vessel shall be placed at a height above the hull not greater than three-quarters of that of the forward masthead light. They shall not be so low as to be interfered with by deck lights.

(h) The sidelights, if in a combined lantern and carried on a power driven vessel of less than 20 metres in length, shall be placed not less than 1 metre below the masthead light.

(i) When the rules prescribe two or three lights to be carried in a vertical line, they shall be spaced as follows:

(i) On a vessel of 20 metres in length or more such lights shall be spaced not less than 2 metres apart, and the lowest of these shall, except where a towing light is required, be placed at a height of not less than 4 metres above the hull.
(ii) On a vessel of less than 20 metres in length such lights shall be spaced not less than 1 metre apart and the lowest of these shall, except where a towing light is required, be placed at a height of not less than 2 metres above the gunwale.
(iii) When three lights are carried they shall be equally spaced.

(j) The lower of the two all-round lights prescribed for a vessel when engaged in fishing shall be at a height above the sidelights not less than twice the distance between the two vertical lights.

(k) The forward anchor light prescribed in Rule 30(a)(i), when two are carried, shall not be less than 4.5 metres above the after one. On a vessel of 50 metres or more in length this forward anchor light shall be placed at a height of not less than 6 metres above the hull.

3. Horizontal positioning and spacing of lights.

(a) When two masthead lights are prescribed for a power driven vessel, the horizontal distance between them shall be not less than one-half of the length of the vessel but need not be more than 100 metres. The forward light shall be placed not more than one-quarter of the length of the vessel from the stern.

(b) On a power-driven vessel of 20 metres or more in length the sidelights shall not be placed in front of the forward masthead lights. They shall be placed at or near the side of the vessel.

(c) When the lights prescribed in Rule 27(b)(i) or Rule 28 are placed vertically between the forward masthead light(s) and the after masthead light(s) these all-round lights shall be placed at a horizontal distance of not less than 2 metres from the fore and aft centreline of the vessel in the athwatrtships direction.

(d) When only one masthead light is prescribed for a power driven vessel, this light shall not be exhibited forward of amidships; except that a vessel of less than 20metres in length need not exhibit this light forward of amidships but shall exhibit it as far forward as practical.

4. Details of location of direction-indicating lights for fishing vessels, dredgers and vessels engaged in underwater operations.

(a) The light indicating the direction of the outlying gear from a vessel engaged in fishing as prescribed in Rule 26(c)(ii) shall be placed at a horizontal distance of not less than 2 metres and not more than 6 metres away from the two all-round red and white lights. This light shall be placed not higher than the all-round white light prescribed in Rule 26(c)(i) and not lower than the sidelights.

(b) The lights and shapes on a vessel engaged in dredging or underwater operations to indicate the obstructed side and/or the side on which it is safe to pass, as prescribed in Rule 27(d)(i) and (ii), shall be placed at the minimum practical horizontal distance, but in no case less than 2 metres, from the lights or shapes prescribed in Rule 27(b)(i) or (ii). In no case shall the upper of these lights or shapes be at a greater height than the lower of the three lights or shapes prescribed in Rule 27(b)(i) or (ii).

5. Screens for sidelights.

The sidelights of vessels of 20 metres or more in length shall be fitted with inboard screens painted matt black, and meeting the requirements of Section 9 of this Annex. On vessels of less than 20 metres in length the sidelights, if necessary to meet the requirements of Section 9 of this Annex, shall be fitted with inboard matt black screens. With a combined lantern, using a single vertical filament and a very narrow division between the green and red sections, external screens need not be fitted.

6. Shapes

(a) Shapes shall be black and of the following size.

(i) A ball shall have a diameter of not less than 0.6 metres.

(ii) A cone shall have a base diameter of not less than 0.6 metres and a height equal to its diameter.

(iii) A cylinder shall have a diameter of at least 0.6 metres and a height of twice its diameter.

(iv) A diamond shape shall consist of two cones as defined in (ii) above having a common base.

(b) The vertical distance between shapes shall be at least 1.5 metres.

(c) In a vessel of less than 20 metres in length shapes of lesser dimensions but commensurate with the size of the vessel may be used and the distance apart may be correspondingly reduced.

7. Colour specification of lights

The chromacity of all navigation lights shall conform to the following standards, which lie within the boundaries of the area of the diagram specified for each colour by the International Commission on Illumination (CIE).

The boundaries of the area for each colour are given by indicating the corner co-ordinates, which are as follows:

(i) White

| x | 0.525 | 0.525 | 0.452 | 0.310 | 0.310 |
| | 0.443 | | | | |

| y | 0.382 | 0.440 | 0.440 | 0.348 | 0.283 |
| | 0.382 | | | | |

(ii) Green

| x | 0.028 | 0.009 | 0.300 | 0.203 |
| y | 0.385 | 0.723 | 0.511 | 0.356 |

(iii) Red

| x | 0.680 | 0.660 | 0.735 | 0.721 |
| y | 0.320 | 0.320 | 0.265 | 0.259 |

(iv) Yellow

| x | 0.612 | 0.618 | 0.575 | 0.575 |
| y | 0.382 | 0.382 | 0.425 | 0.406 |

8. Intensity of lights

(a) The minimum luminous intensity of lights shall be calculated by using the formula:

$$I = 3.43 \times 10^6 \times T \times D^2 \times K^{-D}$$

Where I is luminous intensity in candelas under service conditions

T is threshold factor 2×10^{-7} lux,

K is atmospheric transmissivity

D is range of visibility (luminous range) of the light in nautical miles

For prescribed lights, K shall be 0.8, corresponding to a meteorological visibility of approximately 13 nautical miles.

(b) A selection of figures derived from the formula is given in the following table:

Range of visibility (luminous range) of light in nautical miles (D)	Luminous intensity of light in candelas for K = 0.8 miles
1	0.9
2	4.3
3	12
4	27
5	52
6	94

Note: The maximum luminous intensity of navigation lights should be limited to avoid undue glare. This shall not be achieved by a variable control of the luminous density.

9. Horizontal sectors

(a)
(i) In the forward direction, sidelights as fitted on the vessel shall show the minimum required intensities. The intensities shall decrease to reach practical cut-off between 1 degree and 3 degrees outside the prescribed sectors.

(ii) For sternlights and masthead lights and at 22.5 degrees abaft the beam for sidelights, the minimum required intensities shall be maintained over the arc of the horizon up to 5 degrees within the limits of the sectors prescribed in Rule 21. From 5 degrees within the prescribed sectors the intensity may decrease by 50 per cent up to the prescribed limits; it shall decrease steadily to reach the practical cut-off at not more than 5 degrees outside the prescribed sectors.

(b)
(i) All-round lights shall be so located as not to be obscured by masts, top-masts or structures within angular sectors of more than 6 degrees, except anchor lights prescribed in Rule 30 which need not be placed at an impractical height above the hull.

(ii) If it is impractical to comply with paragraph (b)(i) of this section by exhibiting only one all-round light, two all-round lights shall be used suitably positioned or screened so that they appear, as far as practicable, as one light at a distance of one mile.

10. Vertical sectors

(a) The vertical sectors of electric lights, as fitted, with the exception of lights on sailing vessels underway shall ensure that:

(i) At least the required minimum intensity is maintained at all angles from 5 degrees above to 5 degrees below the horizontal;

(ii) At least 60 percent of the required minimum intensity is maintained from 7.5 degrees above to 7.5 degrees below the horizontal.

(b) In the case of sailing vessels underway the vertical sectors of electric lights as fitted shall ensure that:

(i) At least the required minimum intensity is maintained at all angles from 5 degrees above to 5 degrees below the horizontal;

(ii) At least 50 percent of the required minimum intensity is maintained from 25 degrees above to 25 degrees below the horizontal.

(c) In the case of lights other than electric these specifications shall be met as closely as possible.

11. Intensity of non-electric lights

Non-electric lights shall so far as practicable comply with the minimum intensities, as specified in the Table given in Section 8 of this Annex.

12. Manoeuvring light.

Notwithstanding the provisions of paragraph 2(f) of this Annex the manoeuvring light described in Rule 34(b) shall be placed in the same fore and aft vertical plane as the masthead light or lights and, where practicable, at a minimum height of 2 metres vertically above the forward masthead light, provided that it shall be carried not less than 2 metres vertically above or below the after masthead light. On a vessel where only one mast-head light is carried the manoeuvring light, if fitted, shall be carried where it can best be seen, not less than 2 metres vertically apart from the masthead light.

13. High speed craft

The masthead light of a high speed craft with a length to breadth ratio of less than 3.0 may be placed at a height related to the breadth of the craft lower than that prescribed in paragraph 2(a)(i) of this Annex, provided that the base angle of the isosceles triangles formed by the sidelights and the masthead light, when seen in end elevation, is not less than 27 degrees.

14. Approval

The construction of lights and shapes and the installation of lights on board the vessel shall be to the satisfaction of the appropriate authority of the State whose flag the vessel is entitled to fly.

Annex II
Additional signals for fishing vessels fishing in close proximity

I have never seen these signals in anger – but this section is worth a skim, just in case you do: it will certainly impress your crew if you can nonchalantly identify a purse seiner.

1. General

The lights mentioned herein shall, if exhibited in pursuance of Rule 26(d), be placed where they can best be seen. They shall be at least 0.9 metres apart but at a lower level than lights prescribed in Rule 26(b)(i) and (c)(i). The lights shall be visible all round the horizon at a distance of at least 1 mile but at a lesser distance than the lights prescribed by these rules for fishing vessels.

2. Signals for trawlers.

(a) Vessels when engaged in trawling, whether using demersal or pelagic gear, may exhibit:

(i) When shooting their nets:
Two white lights in a vertical line

(ii)When hauling their nets:
One white light over one red
light in a vertical line

(iii) When the net has come fast
upon an obstruction:
Two red lights in a vertical line.

(b) Each vessel engaged in pair trawling may exhibit:

(i) By night, a searchlight directed forward and in the direction of the other vessel of the pair.

(ii) When shooting or hauling their nets or when their nets have come fast upon an obstruction, the lights prescribed in 2(a) above.

3. Signals for purse seiners

Vessels engaged with purse seine gear may exhibit two yellow lights in a vertical line. These lights shall flash alternately every second and with equal light and occultation duration. These lights may be exhibited only when the vessel is hampered by its fishing gear.

These are inter-fishing boat signals. As a yachtsman – or indeed any form of mariner other than another fisherman, you have no particular need to know when a boat is shooting or hauling its nets. All you need to know is that it is fishing, and that your job is to keep clear.

Let me do my best to explain some of the terms.
● There are 2 sorts of fish, evidently, those that live on or close to the seabed and those that swim in the middle water. The first, seabed fish, are called demersal . And the second, the middle water fish, are pelagic . You can trawl for either.
● Most trawlers pull an open-mouthed net through the water – either along the bottom or in the middle water – using an ingenious arrangement of wires and underwater kites that fly through the water holding the net at the right depth and keeping the net aperture open. Clearly, since the sides of the net are separated by some distance, each is attached to a separate towing wire. In general, one trawler pulls both wires itself.
● Occasionally, however, you find trawlers where each side of the net is pulled by a separate vessel. This is called pair trawling. Rather like a sort of lateral towing, you would be ill-advised to sail between the trawlers. Hence the need to shine a searchlight across the water between the boats.
● More arcane still is purse seining. The fishing vessel uses a net like a vertical curtain, which it deploys in a wide circle. The top of the net is made buoyant by floats and the bottom is weighted. Ideally, the curtain is deployed around a shoal of fish. When the circle is complete, the boat picks up both ends of the net and pulls in on a draw-string which runs along the base of the curtain. This closes off the bottom and forms a sort of vertical 'purse' - with an entire shoal of fish inside. All the fisherman has to do then is to pull the net inboard, freeze the catch, open a can of beer and sail for home as fast as possible.

Mnemonics:
● Shooting its net (ie deploying it). Two white lights are like the blast coming out of a double-barrelled shotgun, i.e. shooting.
● Hauling the nets. The whiter skippers cap over a very red face as he goes through the effort of bringing the nets back inboard.
● Fast on an obstruction. Two reds: beware. Don't come close if you are trawling too.
● Purse seining. The lights resemble yellow buoys bobbing up and down in the water as the purse is drawn tight.

Annex III
Technical details of sound signal appliances

I started off by saying that you should feel free to skip this annex. I would, however, draw your attention to paragraph 1(c), which gives 'typical' ranges at which a foghorn can be heard. Anything between half a mile and 2 miles – and it could be significantly reduced. If you are closing each other at, say 15 knots, that equates to anything between 2 minutes and 8 minutes from first detection by ear and a collision. It is not long.

1. Whistles

(a) Frequencies and range of audibility

The fundamental frequency of the signal shall lie between 70 – 700 Hz.
The range of audibility of the signal from a whistle shall be determined by those frequencies, which may include the fundamental and/or one or more higher frequencies, which lie within the range 180 – 700 Hz (+– 1%) and which provide the sound pressure levels specified in paragraph 1(c) below.

(b) Limits of fundamental frequencies

To ensure a wide variety of whistle characteristics, the fundamental frequency of a whistle shall be between the following limits:
(i) 70 – 200 Hz, for a vessel 200 metres or more in length.
(ii) 130 – 350 Hz, for a vessel 75 metres but less than 200 metres in length.
(iii) 250 – 700 Hz, for a vessel less than 75 metres in length

(c) Sound signal intensity and range of audibility

A whistle fitted in a vessel shall provide, in the direction of maximum intensity of the whistle and at a distance of 1 metre from it, a sound pressure level in at least one 1/3rd-octave band within the range of frequencies 180 – 700 Hz (+/– 1%) of not less than the appropriate figure given in the table below.

The range of audibility in the table below is for information and is approximately the range at which

a whistle may be heard on its forward axis with 90% probability in conditions of still air on board a vessel having average background noise level at the listening posts (taken to be 68 dB in the octave band centred on 250 Hz and 63 dB in the octave band centred on 500 Hz).

In practice the range at which a whistle may be heard is extremely variable and depends critically on weather conditions; the values given can be regarded as typical but under conditions of strong wind or high ambient noise level at the listening post the range may be much reduced.

(d) Directional properties

The sound pressure level of a directional whistle shall be not more than 4 dB below the prescribed sound pressure level on the axis at any direction in the horizontal plane within +/– 45 degrees of the axis. The sound pressure level at any other direction shall not be more than 10 dB below the prescribed sound pressure level on that axis, so that the range in any direction will be at least half the range on the forward axis. The sound pressure level shall be measured in that 1/3rd-octave band which determines the audibility range.

(e) Positioning of whistles

When a directional whistle is to be used as the only whistle on a vessel, it shall be installed with its maximum intensity directed straight ahead.

A whistle shall be placed as high as practicable on a vessel, in order to reduce interception of the emitted sound by obstructions and also to minimise hearing damage risk to personnel. The sound pressure level of a vessel's own signal at listening posts shall not exceed 110 dB (A) and so far as is practicable should not exceed 100 dB (A).

(f) Fitting of more than 1 whistle

If whistles are fitted at a distance apart of more than 100 metres, it shall be so arranged that they are not sounded simultaneously.

Length of vessel in metres	1/3rd-octave band level at 1 metre in dB referred to 2×10^{-5} N/m^2	Audibility range in nautical miles
200 or more	143	2
75 but less than 200	138	1.5
20 but less than 75	130	1
Less than 20	120	0.5

(g) Combined whistle systems

If due to the presence of obstructions the sound field of a single whistle or of one of the whistles referred to in paragraph 1(f) above is likely to have a zone of greatly reduced signal level, it is recommended that a combined whistle system be fitted so as to overcome this reduction. For the purposes of the Rules, a combined whistle system is to be regarded as a single whistle. The whistles of a combined system should be located at a distance apart of not more than 100 metres and arranged to be sounded simultaneously. The frequency of any one whistle shall differ from those of the others by at least 10Hz.

2. Bell or gong

(a) Intensity of signal

A bell or gong, or other device having similar sound characteristics shall produce a sound pressure level of not less than 110 dB at a distance of 1 metre from it.

(b) Construction

Bells and gongs shall be made of corrosion-resistant material and designed to give a clear tone. The diameter of the mouth of the bell shall not be less than 300 mm for vessels of 20 metres or more in length, and shall be not less than 200 mm for vessels of 12 metres or more but of less than 20 metres in length. Where practicable, a power-driven bell-striker is recommended to ensure constant force but manual operation shall be possible. The mass of the striker shall be not less than 3% of the mass of the bell.

3. Approval

The construction of sound signal appliances, their performance and their installation onboard the vessel shall be to the satisfaction of the appropriate authority of the State whose flag the vessel is entitled to fly.

Section 9 Annex IV Distress signals

Read this and take it in. It is important.

1. The following signals, used or exhibited either together or separately, indicate distress and need of assistance:

(a) A gun or other explosive signal fired at intervals of about a minute.

(b) Continuous sounding with any fog-signalling apparatus.

(c) Rockets or shells, throwing red stars, fired one at a time, at short intervals.

(d) A signal made by radiotelephony or by any other signalling method consisting of the group
••• — — — ••• (SOS) in the Morse Code.

(e) A signal sent by radiotelephony consisting of the spoken word 'Mayday'.

(f) The international code signals of distress indicated by 'NC'.

(g) A signal consisting of a square flag having above or below it a ball, or anything resembling a ball.

(h) Flames on the vessel (as from a burning tar barrel, oil barrel, etc).

(i) A rocket parachute flare or hand flare showing a red light.

(j) A smoke signal giving off orange-coloured smoke.

(k) Slowly and repeatedly raising and lowering arms outstretched to each side.

(l) The radiotelgraph alarm signal.

(m) The radiotelephone alarm signal.

(n) Signals transmitted by Emergency Position-Indicating Radio Beacons.

(o) Approved signals transmitted by radiocommunication systems.

2. The use or exhibition of any of the foregoing signals except for the purpose of indicating distress and need of assistance and the use of other signals which may be confused with any of the above signals is prohibited.

3. Attention is drawn to the relevant sections of the International Code of Signals, the Merchant Ship Search and Rescue Manual and the following signals:

(a) A piece of orange-coloured canvas with either a black square and circle or other appropriate symbol (for identification from the air).

(b) A dye marker.

10 Self-test

Q1

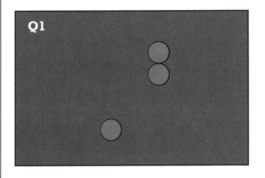

a. What is this vessel?
b. What sound signal would it make in restricted visibility, and how often?
c. What other sorts of vessels would make the same signal?

A1

a. A vessel not under command, making way, viewed from the port bowlight quadrant.

b. The signal (- • •) at intervals of not more than 2 minutes.

c. **N**ot under command, **R**estricted in ability to manoeuvre, vessel **C**onstrained by its draught, **S**ailing vessel, vessel **E**ngaged in fishing, vessel engaged in **T**owing or pushing.

'**N**o **R**adar **C**an **S**ee **E**very **T**arget'

Q2

You are completely lost in thick fog after one of the crew tripped and spilled a bowl of steaming mulligatawny soup over the GPS. Sadly, it also soaked your Rule of the Road book, which has now become completely illegible, despite a gently appealing aroma of curry.

Somewhere in the impenetrable mists ahead of you, you hear: 3 distinct rings on a bell, 5 seconds ringing on a bell, 3 distinct rings on a bell.

a. What is it?
b. How often would you expect the signal to be repeated?
c. Is this noise generated at the bow or the stern of the vessel?

A2

a. A vessel aground, less than 100 metres in length, but over 12 metres in length.

b. Intervals of not more than 1 minute.

c. The bow. Vessels longer than 100 metres would sound a gong after the bell signal, in the after part of the vessel.

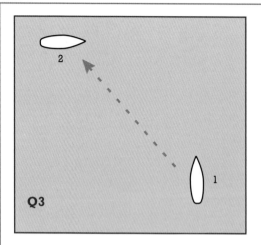

b. In what way is the give-way vessel most likely to alter?
c. What sound signal must the give-way vessel make as he makes this alteration (assuming that the vessels are in sight of each other)?

A3

a. The power driven canoe (2) is the give-way vessel: the ducks will have to wait a moment longer.
b. You would expect him to make a bold alteration of course to starboard.
c. One short blast – the manoeuvring sound signal for altering course to starboard.

(1) = you in a power driven pleasure craft
(2) = power driven canoe on a duck-hunting expedition. It is making way, and on a steady bearing
a. Which is the give-way vessel?

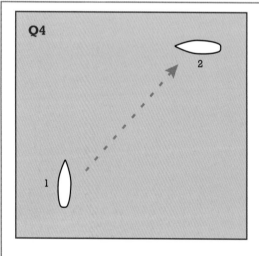

c. What must the stand-on vessel do initially?
d. At what stage **may** it take action to avoid a collision?
e. When **must** it act?

A4

a. The other vessel is the stand-on vessel. You must give way to him.
b. A vessel motor-sailing should show a black cone apex downwards, shown in the forward part of the vessel where it can best be seen.
c. As the stand-on vessel, the other craft should maintain its course and speed.
d. The stand-on vessel **may** act as soon as it becomes apparent that the other vessel is not taking appropriate action.
e. The stand on vessel **must** act when she finds her self so close to the other vessel that a collision cannot be avoided by the action of the give-way vessel alone.

(1) = you in a power driven vessel
(2) = sailing boat which is motor-sailing, making way, and on a steady bearing
Both vessels are in sight of each other.
a. Which is the give-way vessel?
b. What shape should the other vessel be showing?

Q5

You decide to go for a career change and throw in your multi-million pound banking job in the City to become a trawler man. You buy an old North Sea trawler, called the 'WHITE ELEPHANT', which leaks like a sieve and is 62 metres long. Some weeks later, you pluck up the courage to go out for your first day's fishing.

a. What shape must you show when trawling by day?
b. It gets dark: you are making way and engaged in trawling. What lights do you show?
c. You come across a vessel towing that is not showing Restricted in Ability to Manoeuvre shapes: should you keep out of his way, or vice versa?

A5

a. The 'fish' shape: 2 cones, apex together, in a vertical line one above the other.

b. • All-round green over all-round white.
   • A masthead steaming light, higher than, and abaft the green light (> 50 metres).
   • Sidelights and a stern light (but only when making way – which is just about the whole time when trawling).

c. The towing vessel should keep out of the fishing vessel's way. If, however, the towing vessel was RAM, it would be the other way round.

Q6

You are a passenger on a small ferry crossing the Chesapeake Bay on a dark and stormy night. Suddenly there is a loud bang, and you look up to see that everyone on the bridge has been stunned by an explosion on the steering control box. The ferry is careering all over the place. On investigation you discover that you are the only person onboard with any knowledge of Rule of the Road.

a. What lights should you show, and why?
b. If it was daytime, what shapes would you be hoisting?
c. To compound your problems, the chief engineer arrives on the bridge and says that the main engines have stopped: should you adjust your lights or not?

A6

a. You are a vessel not under command, making way. Therefore you should show:
   • Two red all-round lights, one above the other, where they can best be seen (usually at or close to the masthead).
   • Sidelights and stern light.
   • Turn off the masthead steaming lights.
b. Two black balls in a vertical line where they can best be seen.
c. You are now a vessel not under command, under way but not making way. Therefore, you no longer need to show sidelights and a stern light: the two all-round reds are sufficient.

Q7

You come across a vessel with this flag hoist.

a. What are the flags?
b. What is it trying to tell you?
c. Are there any other flag/shapes which would convey the same message?
d. Name the two sound signals which would mean the same?

   • A square flag with a ball (or something resembling a ball) either above or below it.
   • A flag signal 'S O S'

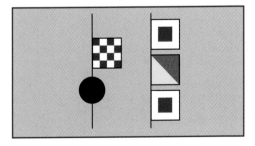

A7

a. The flags are 'NOVEMBER CHARLIE'.
b. This is a distress signal.
c. There are in all 15 listed distress signals, but the other 2 distress signals involving flags and shapes are:

d. • A gun or other explosive device at intervals of about 1 minute.
   • Continuous sounding of a fog signal.

Q8

You are sailing down the Solent on a sunny afternoon when you see, approaching from the southeast at high speed, a merchant ship with a cylinder hoisted in its rigging. The crew think that this hoist means that there is a pilot embarked.

a. Are they right?
b. If not, what does it mean?
c. Can you impose your right of way as a sailing vessel?
d. What should you do?

A8

a. No. They are wrong.
b. This is the signal for a vessel constrained by its draught
c. No: all vessels except those restricted in their ability to manoeuvre, and not under command must avoid impeding a vessel constrained by its draught.
d. Anything at all as long as you get out of his way and let him know you are doing it. The quickest way would be to turn 90° to its track and open the range that way.

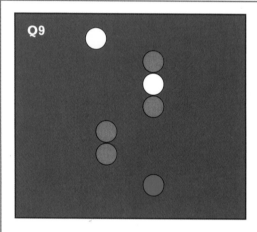

a. What is it?
b. Which side should you pass?
c. Other than 'not very good looking', what would it look like by day?

A9

a. A dredger, or a vessel engaged in underwater operations, restricted in its ability to manoeuvre.
It is making way, less than 50 metres in length and you are looking at it from its starboard bowlight quadrant. An obstruction exists on its starboard side (ie this side).
b. Certainly not this side: try the port side.
c. By day it would look like this:

Q10

You are in a small motor boat in fog, eyes glued to the radar set. On the radar screen, you see a contact closing on a steady bearing from a relative bearing 45° on the starboard bow. Its range is now 2 miles.

a. What should you do?
b. What manoeuvring sound signal should you make?
c. What reaction would you expect from the other vessel?

A10

a. Provided that it does not interfere with other shipping, alter course to starboard to put the vessel on your port bow.
b. None in restricted visibility unless you are in sight of the other vessel (which you aren't): you just carry on making the standard fog signals.
c. Alter course to starboard too to put you on his port beam, or even his port quarter.

Q11

You have just picked up your new sailing boat 'LAME DUCK' from a second-hand car salesman in Dover and you decide to go to France for an afternoon of wine and seafood, crossing the Dover Straits separation scheme in the process. She is 15 metres in length. It is a clear day, but the wind is not strong enough to sail, so you are forced to rely on your totally unreliable 1950s lawn mower engine for propulsion.

a. You meet the separation lane traffic flow from your port beam: should you give way or stand on?
b. A short while after, you meet the traffic flow from your starboard beam. Should you give way or stand on?
c. In the separation zone, between the two lanes, you come across a trawler. Is it fishing legally, according to the rules? Could it fish in the lanes themselves?

A11

a. You give way. Vessels less than 20 metres in length, or sailing vessels, should not impede the safe passage of a power-driven vessel following a traffic lane.
b. Ditto.
c. A fishing vessel can fish in a separation zone.
   It can also fish in the separation lanes provided that it does not impede the safe passage of a power driven vessel following a separation lane.

Q12

a. What lights does a pilot vessel show when under way?
b. What shapes does it show by day?
c. What sound signal is made by a pilot vessel under way?

A12

a. Side lights, stern light and two all-round masthead lights, white over red.
b. You will see the word 'P I L O T' on her side and she flies a pilot flag, divided horizontally into 2 halves: white over red.
c. One prolonged blast at intervals of not more than 2 minutes.
   May also sound 4 short blasts to identify her as a pilot vessel.

Q13

You are sailing your antique second-hand boat 'LAME DUCK' back from an abortive trip to France after one of your crew found that he was allergic to mussels. The wind is fair, and you are able to give your motor a rest. You are well clear of the separation schemes.
a. You encounter a vessel engaged in fishing: who has right of way?
b. Your crew is keen to anchor for lunch south of the Isle of Wight in order to relish the decomposing cheese that you bought in the supermarket. What shape should you hoist?
c. Your anchor starts dragging: are you technically under way, or made fast?

A13

a. Sailing vessels must keep clear of fishing vessels: so you keep out of his way.
b. A single black ball in the fore part of the boat.
c. You are technically under way.

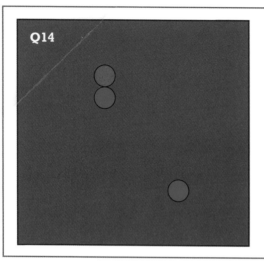

a. What is this?
b. Is the engine being used?
c. You are in a motor boat and you come across this guy at night on a steady bearing, one mile away and 30° on your port bow. What should you do?

A14
a. A sailing vessel viewed from the starboard bow light quadrant.
b. No. If it were, the vessel would show the lights of a power driven vessel.
c. It depends: you must give way. You could:
   • Slow down and let him pass ahead.
   • Alter course to port to pass under his stern.
   • Put him very much broader on your port side by altering to starboard, trying to overtake him.

Q15
Discovering a magic turn of speed in your trawler 'WHITE ELEPHANT', you decide to waste no time returning to harbour to put the total day's catch on the market. Two fish. On the way, you find that you overhaul your great rival, Hal Ibut, in his brand new vessel just as you enter the channel to your home port. Visibility is good, but unfortunately your VHF set is broken.
a. You want to overtake him by passing down his starboard side. How could you signal that?
b. He is happy. What is his reply
c. So you decide to overtake. Just as you are

pulling abeam of him, Hal alters course hard to starboard to avoid his Scottish crewman, Mac Arel, who has fallen overboard after drinking too much whisky. Who is responsible for collision avoidance?

A15
a. Make the sound signal (− − ·) to show that you want to overtake to starboard.
b. He makes the signal (− · − ·) to show that he is happy.
c. You are unequivocally responsible for keeping out of his way until you are finally past and clear: in theory, he could manoeuvre as much as he likes.

Q16
You are in a sailing boat, with the wind from right astern. Your boom is out on the starboard side.
a. You are going so fast that you overtake a powerboat who, in turning round to admire your breath-taking turn of speed, swerves towards you. Who is responsible for taking keeping clear?
b. Your heartbeat is beginning to recover when you meet another sailing boat on a steady bearing close hauled, approaching you on the starboard tack. Who has to give way?
c. No sooner has he passed, than a second sailing vessel approaches you on the close-hauled port tack with a cone, apex downwards in the rigging. Who gives way now?

A16
a. You are responsible for collision avoidance as the overtaking vessel, despite the fact that he is a powerboat.
b. You are on different tacks. Regrettably, you are on the port tack and he is on starboard. Therefore, you must give way to him.
c. The fact that he is on the port tack and close-hauled is irrelevant: he is technically a power driven vessel, and so must give way to you. If he was not operating his engine, he would be more close hauled than you, so you would have had to give way.

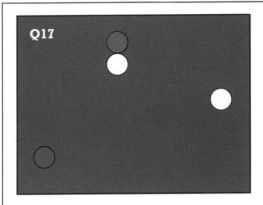

a. Tell me all you can about this vessel.
b. Can you safely pass on any side?
c. By day, what 2 shapes would it carry?

A17

a. It is a vessel engaged in fishing other than trawling, viewed from the starboard bow light quadrant.
It has gear outlying at least 150 metres in the direction of the white light, and the green sidelight indicates that it is making way.
b. Yes, but avoid passing close in the direction of the white light: if possible go round the back.

c.

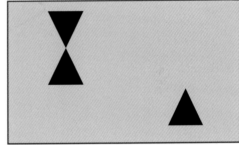

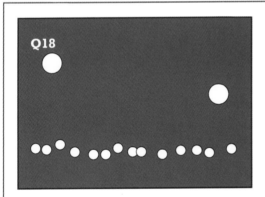

a. What is this?
b. What can you say about its length?
c. Is its bow to the right or the left?

A18

a. A vessel at anchor.
b. Not much for sure. However, the fact that it has 2 anchor lights indicates that it may be longer than 50 metres, and the working lights on the upper deck are compulsory for vessels greater than 100 m in length, optional for shorter vessels.
c. To the left.

Q19
You are appointed to command the tugboat 'INCAPABLE', 57 metres long and, despite the fact that she is 75 years old, she is your first command and you are proud of her. You are contracted to tow a consignment of coals to Newcastle. You are not restricted in your ability to manoeuvre.
a. You decide to measure the length of the tow: where do you measure it from and to?
b. The length is 206 m. What shapes do you show?
c. What lights do you need at night?

A19
a. From the stern of the towing vessel to the stern of the final vessel in the tow.
b. When the tow is longer than 200 metres, a diamond shape where best seen on the tug, and also on the tow.
c. Three masthead lights in a vertical line. A further masthead light higher than and abaft the forward three.
Sidelights, stern light and yellow towing light.

Vessels being towed show sidelights and a sternlight.

Q20

You are still master of the antique 57-metre tug 'INCAPABLE', towing the load of coals to Newcastle. Your tow is 206 metres in length. You are not restricted in your ability to manoeuvre.

a. In restricted visibility, what sound signal would you make, and how often?

b. What signal would the final vessel in the tow make, and how often?

A20

a. (— · ·) at intervals not exceeding 2 minutes.

b. If manned, the final vessel in the tow makes (— · · ·) at intervals not exceeding 2 minutes, where possible directly after the signal made by the tug.

Q21

a. What signals does a vessel constrained by its draught make in restricted visibility?

b. Can a sailing vessel be constrained by its draught?

c. What lights does it show by night?

d. What shape does it display by day?

A21

a. (— · ·) at intervals not exceeding 2 minutes.

b. A vessel constrained by its draught must be a power driven vessel.

c. Three all-round red lights in a vertical line where they can best be seen, masthead steaming lights, sidelights and a sternlight.

d.

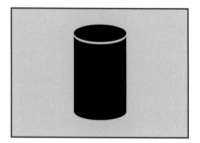

Q22

You are navigating a narrow channel in the Norwegian Fjords. You are in a large power driven bulk carrier with a cargo of high-quality aquavit that would go aground (and cheer up the locals immensely) if it left the channel.

a. Which side of the channel should you keep as a matter of course?

b. A vessel approaches from your starboard bow, crossing the channel. It is nearly on a steady bearing. Should you alter to avoid it?

c. You approach a blind corner. What signal do you make? If there is anyone the other side of the corner, how would he reply?

A22

a. Starboard.

b. If necessary, yes. But as a crossing vessel, it should not impede your passage.

c. One prolonged blast. He would reply with one prolonged blast also.

Q23

a. When should navigation lights be shown (3 occasions)?

b. What lights in general should a yacht's tender show when propelled by oars?

A23

a.
- Between sunset and sunrise.
- Restricted visibility
- All other circumstances when it might be necessary.

b. A white electric torch or lighted lantern.

Q24
Name the 6 categories of 'Restricted in Ability to Manoeuvre'.

A24
- A vessel engaged in laying, servicing or picking up a **N**avigation mark, submarine cable or pipeline.
- A vessel engaged in dredging, surveying or **U**nderwater operations.
- A vessel engaged in **R**eplenishment or transferring persons, provisions or cargo while underway.
- A vessel engaged in launching or recovery of **A**ircraft.
- A vessel engaged in **M**ineclearance operations.
- A vessel engaged in **T**owing operations that seriously restricts the towing vessel and tow in their ability to deviate from their course.

'**Never Use RAM T**houghtlessly'

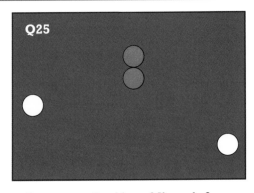

Q25

a. Do you envy the skipper? If so, why?
b. Which is its forward end?
c. What sound signal would he make in fog?

A25
a. Not particularly. He is aground.
b. The forward end is the one with the higher of the two white all-round lights.
c. 3 distinct rings on a bell, 5 seconds rapid ringing, and 3 distinct rings. Repeated every minute.

If longer than 100 metres in length, this will be followed by 5 seconds sounding of a gong aft.

Q26
a. Is 'Not Under Command' a distress signal?
b. What shapes should a diving boat show if it cannot sensibly display RAM shapes?
c. What shapes are shown by a vessel aground?

A26
a. No.

b. A rigid 'Flag Alpha'

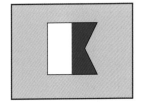

c. Three black balls in a vertical line

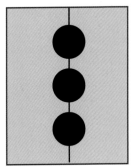

Q27
a. What lights will a vessel show when pushing ahead?
b. What will the vessels being pushed ahead show?
c. Is there any difference if they are pushed ahead or towed alongside?

A27
a. 2 masthead lights in a vertical line. Sidelights and sternlight. A third masthead light if required, abaft and above the forward lights.
b. Sidelights only.
c. Yes. Vessels being towed alongside also show a sternlight.

Q28
a. Where do the rules apply?
b. Can they me modified locally?
c. What is the definition of 'a short blast'?
d. What is the definition of a 'prolonged blast'?

A28
a. On the high seas and in all waters connected therewith navigable by seagoing vessels, except where modified by local rules.
b. Yes.
c. A blast of about 1 second's duration.
d. A blast of 4 – 6 seconds' duration.

Q29
You are entering Baltimore Harbour in your 120-foot superyacht. It is a beautiful sunny day. The paparazzi are out in force, admiring your filmstar looks and those of your partner. There are boats everywhere.

a. You have to turn to port: what manoeuvring signal do you make?
b. One of the paparazzi boats makes 3 short blasts: what does this mean?
c. You are worried that someone is getting in your way. Is there a sound signal you can make to tell him to keep clear?

A29
a. Two short blasts.
b. It is operating astern propulsion.
c. At least 5 short and rapid blasts on the whistle.

Q30
You are in a small motor boat without radar and the fog is so thick that you have just lost your coffee mug in the cockpit.

a. You hear a fog signal ' — • •' from forward of the beam. What could it be?
b. Do you have to accord it any special priority?
c. You are under way, making way. What signal do you make, and how often?

A30
a.
• NUC
• Constrained by draught
• RAM
• Sailing boat
• Vessel engaged in fishing
• Vessel towing or pushing.

b. No. In fog, every vessel has to take its own avoiding action. These are, however, vessels to keep especially clear of.
c. One prolonged blast at intervals of not more than 2 minutes.

Q31

a. Sketch a northerly cardinal buoy, including colours, topmark and light characteristics.

b. Which side must you pass it?

c. Do the same for a westerly cardinal buoy.

d. And an easterly cardinal.

A31

a.

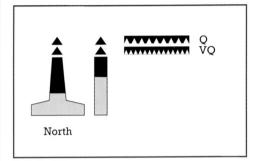

North

b. You must pass to the north of it.

c.

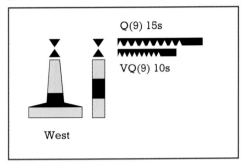

Q(9) 15s

VQ(9) 10s

West

d.

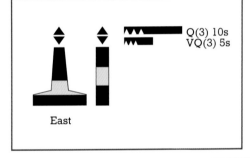

Q(3) 10s

VQ(3) 5s

East

Q32

a. What is the difference between 'under way' and 'making way'?

b. What lights does a non-displacement vessel show when under way?

c. What lights would you expect to see from a police boat?

A32

a.
- 'Under way' means not at anchor or attached to the shore.
- A vessel is 'making way' when it is moving through the water.

b. Standard lights for a power driven vessel. Plus an all-round flashing yellow light

c. Standard lights for a power driven vessel. Plus an all-round flashing blue light (when required).

Q33

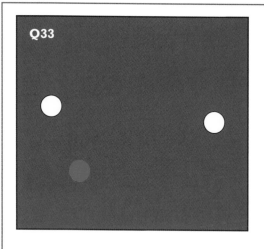

a. What is it?
b. How long is it?
c. If it is approaching you on a steady
   bearing from your port bow in open
   water, what do you do?

A33
a. A power driven vessel under way,
   viewed from the starboard navigation
   light quadrant.
b. From the lights, it could be any length.
c. Stand on.

Q34
a. From what relative bearing is an
   approaching vessel considered to
   be overtaking?
b. Over what arcs do the sidelights shine?
c. Are you authorised to set off distress
   flares to celebrate your great aunt's
   good fortune in winning the
   National Lottery?

A34
a. It is considered to be overtaking
   when approaching from within the
   arc of the stern light. ie from further
   aft than 22.5 degrees abaft the beam.
b. From the bow to 22.5 degrees abaft
   each respective beam.
c. No.

Q35

You are in a power driven vessel in good visibility, proceeding along a busy shipping lane. You find that you are steadily overtaking a vessel on your port bow, at a range of about half a mile. On your starboard quarter there is a third vessel, which is not overtaking, but making about the same course and speed as you, about three quarters of a mile distant:

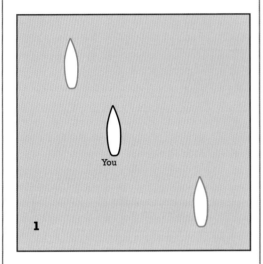

1

Suddenly, the vessel on your port bow swerves 75° to starboard:

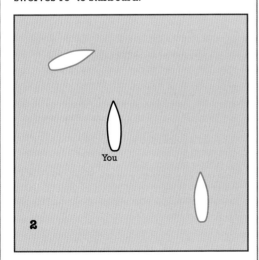

2

What should you do?

A35

You are bound to keep clear of the vessel being overtaken, no matter what he does.

However, if you alter to starboard to keep clear of him, you will be crossing the third vessel's bows – and since you are on his port bow, he would be the stand-on vessel. Turning to starboard would therefore be a dangerous manoeuvre:

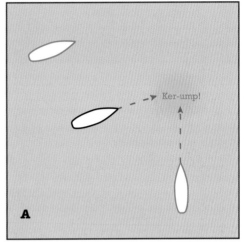

A

You could stop or slow down in order to let them all sort themselves out. You might then choose to come a little bit to port to clear the first vessel's stern:

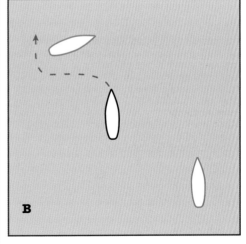

B

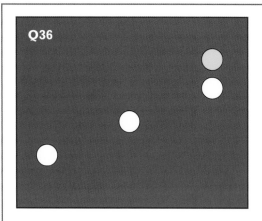

Q36

a. What is it?
b. What would you hear in fog?

A36

a. A tug and tow, with 2 vessels in tow, viewed from the stern light quadrant on the starboard side.
b. The tug would make a signal (— · ·) every 2 minutes. If the last vessel in the tow is manned, it would follow this with a further signal (— · · ·).

Q37
You are 10 miles offshore on a coastal passage by night in good visibility.

You see, some way from you, a single white light. Name 3 things that it could be?

A37
- A vessel's stern light
- A vessel at anchor
- A masthead light, hull-down
- The working lights of a fishing vessel (this is not in the rules, but in reality a very likely source of the light).
- Dracone under tow.

It might also be a shore light.
I am embarrassed to say that once, when there was an indistinct horizon, I mistook a bright, low altitude star for a ship closing on a steady bearing.

Q38
You are in fog (again). After a long night on the helm you get your head down, leaving the morning watch to your father-in-law, a retired naval stoker who has recently become a little hard of hearing. Twenty seconds after you drop off, he comes below and gives you a shake, saying that he has heard a fog signal out there. When asked what it was, he says he couldn't say exactly, but it was one of 3 possible signals. Namely:

a. · · · · ·

b. — · · ·

c. · · · ·

What could the vessel be, and at what interval should each signal be sounded?

A38

a. It is unlikely to be this one. This is the 'please get out of my way' signal used only when vessels are in sight of each other. Signalled whenever necessary.
b. Could be this. This is the fog signal used by the last vessel in a tow, when manned. It is sounded every 2 minutes, as far as practical immediately after the (— · ·) of the towing vessel.
c. A pilot vessel on pilotage duty. Sounded whenever necessary to identify it as a pilot vessel. It is used in addition to the standard sound signal for the vessel itself.

Q39

a. What is the difference in the lights shown by a vessel aground and a vessel not under command, not making way?

b. What is the difference between a cone apex up and a cone apex down?

c. Name 2 things that show a shape consisting of 2 cones, apex together.

A39

a.
A vessel aground:

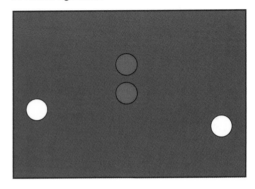

A vessel not under command, not making way:

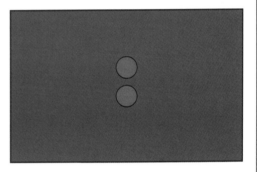

b.
- Cone apex up is a fishing vessel with gear extending more than 150 metres in the direction of the cone.
- Cone apex down is a sailing vessel manoeuvring under power.

c.
- Fishing vessel (or trawler)
- Westerly cardinal buoy topmark

Q40

In Europe, you are entering harbour (with the flood stream). You see a green buoy.

a. Which side do you leave it?

b. What shape is it likely to be?

c. What numbers will it carry: odd or even?

d. If you were in the United States, which side would you leave it, would it be odd or even numbered, and what shape would it be?

A40

a. To starboard.

b. Conical.

c. Odd.

d. To port ('Red - Right - Returning'). It would also have an odd number and be of a rectangular can shape.

Q41

You own a powerboat and decide to go on holiday down the coast with another family in their boat. Two days into the trip, the other boat reports a major engine problem and asks you to tow him back to your home marina.

a. With the tow hitched up, what lights and shapes should you display?

b. If this is impractical, what lights may you display?

c. How many drinks does he owe you when you get home?

A41

a. Unless the tow exceeds 200 m, no shapes. By night, you show standard lights for a power driven vessel plus a second masthead light, directly under the first, and an additional stern light, coloured yellow. He shows side lights and a stern light.

b. Do everything possible to indicate the existence of the tow, and in particular illuminate the towline. In this case, you should show standard steaming lights.

c. Stacks.

Q42

a. In US waters, when entering harbour, do you keep the green buoys to port or starboard?

b. How will you know in the US that you are proceeding from the International COLREGs to the Internal Waters Rules?

c. What does a safe water mark look like?

A42

a. Port. (Red – Right – Returning.)

b. A 'COLREGS Demarcation Line' has been established by the USCG and is generally marked on official US charts.

c.

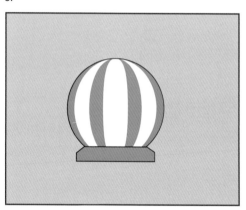

Q43

It is thick fog and you are motoring along, keeping an eye on your radar. On the screen there is a vessel approaching you from your starboard quarter – on a steady bearing at green 160. 'No need to alter,' says Dumbo the mate, 'he is the overtaking vessel.'

a. Is he right?

b. If not, what should you do?

c. The debate continues. Eventually, the other vessel emerges from the mist at half a mile's range. What should you do now?

A43

a. No. Unless you can see the other vessel, the 'overtaking rule' does not apply.

b. This is one occasion when you should alter to port. The rule for restricted visibility says that you shouldn't alter towards a vessel on your beam or abaft it.

c. When it does emerge from the mist it becomes the overtaking vessel: you should then stand on and let him take the appropriate action.

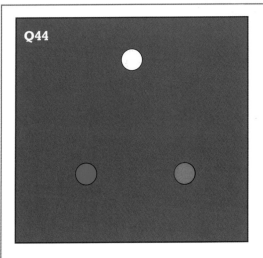

Q44

a. What is it?
b. How long is it?
c. Tough question: is there any way it
   could be longer than this?

A44

a. A power driven vessel less than 50 metres
   in length, coming straight at you.

b. Less than 50 metres in length.

c. It could be longer than 50 metres:
   warships, for instance, sometimes
   show only one masthead steaming
   light, even when they are longer than
   50 metres.

In the real world it might also be a larger ship
with one masthead steaming light defective.

Q45

a. Can you be arrested for infractions
   of the rules?
b. Are you allowed to proceed down a
   separation lane the wrong way?
c. Are you allowed to anchor in a narrow
   channel or fairway?
d. Or fish?

A45

a. Yes.
b. No. The only vessels that are authorised
   to do this are those engaged in the
   maintenance of safety of navigation, or
   those laying, servicing or picking up a
   submarine cable.
c. Only *in extremis*. The rules say that
   vessels '...shall, if the circumstances
   of the case admit, avoid anchoring in
   a narrow channel or fairway.'
d. Yes. Vessels may fish but should avoid
   impeding vessels that are restricted to
   the narrow channel.

Q46

a. How close to a mine countermeasures
   vessel can you go?
b. What lights would it show by night
   (assuming that it is less than 50 metres in
   length and engaged in mine clearance
   operations under way)?
c. What are the corresponding shapes
   by day?

A46

a. 1000 metres when the vessel is engaged
   in mineclearance operations.
b. Lights for a power driven vessel.
   (one masthead steaming light in this
   case) and 3 all-round green lights:
   one at the masthead, and one at
   each yardarm.
c. A ball at the masthead, and one
   at each yardarm.

Q47

a. What is the colour scheme of an isolated danger buoy, including topmarks, lights and shape

b. Who must a seaplane give way to (when on the water)?

c. Should you show anchor lights in your yacht when you have picked up a buoy?

A47

a. Light: group flashing white (2). No particular shape.

b. Everyone. But when in a close quarters situation on the water, it should behave like a power driven vessel.

c. Yes, if it will help collision avoidance.

Q48

a. Name the 2 sorts of shape that you require on a sailing boat.

b. When would you use each one?

c. Which is the least embarrassing vessel to run aground in: an 11-metre yacht or a 15-metre yacht?

A48

a, b. A black ball – used when at anchor. A black cone – hoisted apex down when motor-sailing.

c. Both are pretty embarrassing, to be honest. However, if you run aground in a 15-metre yacht, you must show the correct lights and shapes. Anything less than 12 metres need not.

Q49

a. What is the difference between a vessel towing with one additional masthead light, and a vessel towing with two additional masthead lights?

b. What additional lights would a lifeboat show?

c. What signal can a vessel at anchor make if it is concerned whether another vessel has seen it?

A49

a. You have one additional masthead light if the length of the tow is less than 200 metres. You have 2 if it is longer than 200 metres.

b. A blue flashing light (when on duty).

c. The sound signal (· – ·)

Q50

Spell out the 'hierarchy rule'.

A50

When vessels are in sight of each other, and not counting special rules relating to separation schemes, narrow channels and overtaking, the heirachy is:

- A vessel RAM, NUC or Constrained By its Draught.
- A vessel fishing
- A sailing vessel
- A power driven vessel

11 Quiz cards

Cut out these cards and use them to test yourself or your crew.

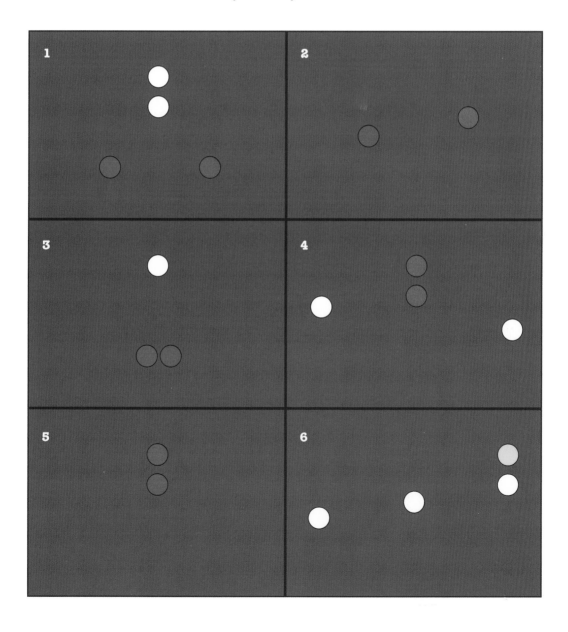

2
Lights of
a sailing vessel, sailing,
seen from right ahead.

1
Lights of
a power driven vessel
seen from right ahead.

4
Lights of
a ship aground
seen from the port beam.

3
Lights of
a sailing boat, motoring,
seen from right ahead or
a small powerboat from ahead.

6
Lights of
a tug towing two other vessels
seen from the starboard quarter.

5
Lights of
a vessel not under command
not making way.

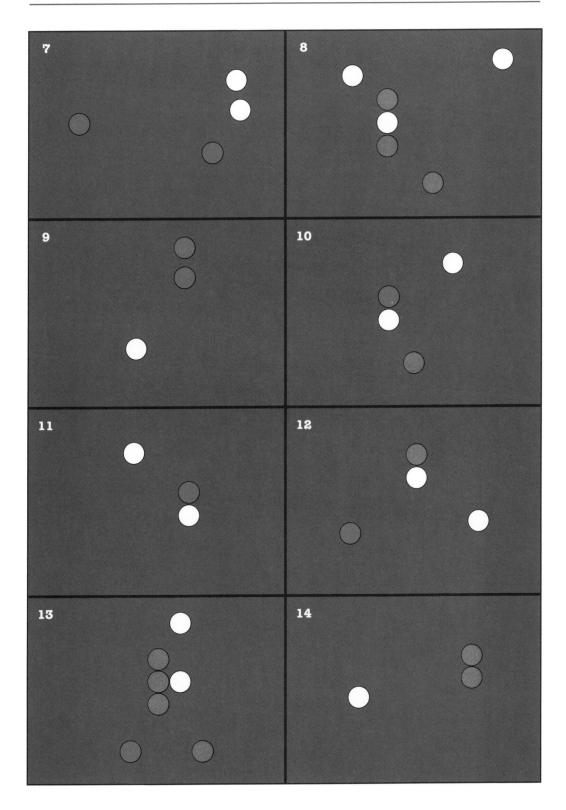

8
Lights of
a vessel restricted in its
ability to manoeuvre
seen from the port beam.

7
Lights of
a tug towing a single vessel
seen from the starboard bow.
The tug is less than
50 metres in length.
The tow is less than
200 metres in length.

10
The lights of
a vessel trawling
seen from the port bow.
Vessel is making way.

9
The lights of
a sailing vessel seen from
the starboard quarter.

12
The lights of a vessel engaged
in fishing (not trawling)
seen from the starboard beam
with outlying gear extending
more than 150 metres in the
direction of the single white light.
Vessel is making way
through the water.

11
The lights of
a vessel trawling
seen from the starboard bow.
Vessel is not making way.

14
The lights of
a vessel aground.
Vessel is less than
50 metres in length.

13
The lights of
a vessel constrained by its draught,
seen from right ahead.

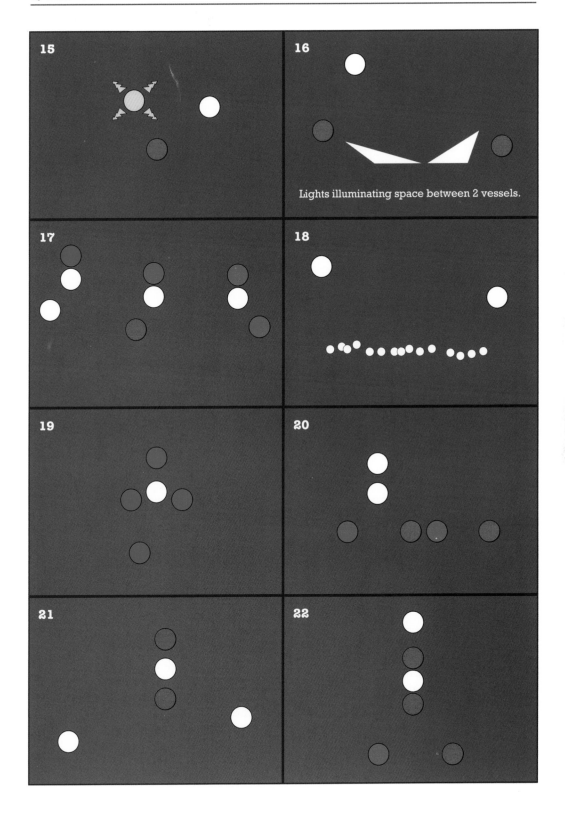

Lights illuminating space between 2 vessels.

16
The lights of
a vessel, that is not normally
engaged in towing,
towing another vessel
in need of assistance.

15
The lights of
an air cushion vessel
(e.g. hovercraft)
seen from the port bow.

18
The lights of
a vessel at anchor.
Seen from the port side
(with deck working lights).

17
The lights of 3 trawlers, all making way.
All are less than 50 metres in length.
From left to right:
• Seen from the starboard quarter.
• Seen from the port beam.
• Seen from the starboard bow.

20
The lights of
a vessel towing another
alongside her port side
seen from right ahead.
The tug is less than
50 metres in length.

19
The lights of
a mine clearance vessel
seen from the starboard bow.
Vessel is under way.

22
The lights of
a vessel restricted in its
ability to manoeuvremaking way
seen from right ahead.
The vessel is less than
50 metres in length.

21
The lights of
a vessel restricted in her ability
to manoeuvre at anchor.
Seen from her starboard side.
The vessel is less than 100 metres
in length (because she has
not illuminated her decks).

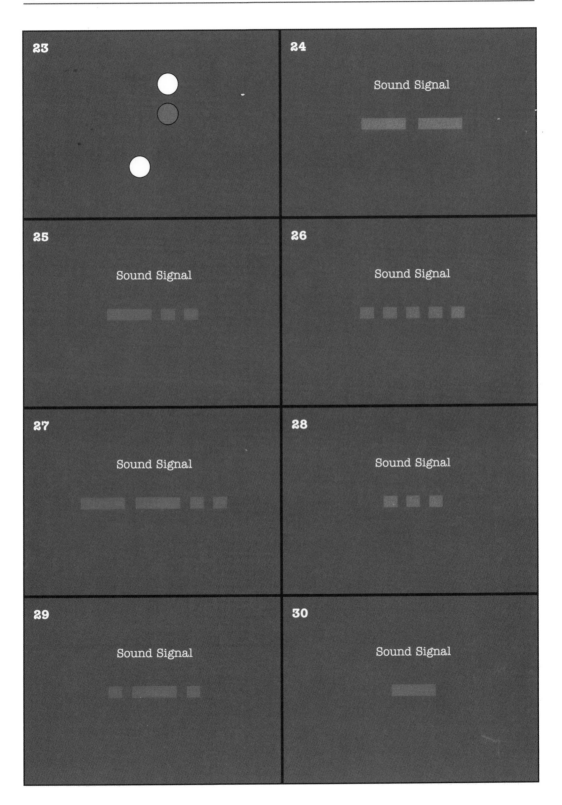

24
The sound signal made
in restricted visibility by
a power driven vessel underway
but stopped in the water.

It is made every 2 minutes.

23
The lights of
a pilot vessel on pilotage
duty underway seen
from the starboard quarter.

26
The sound signal made
when in sight of another vessel
when one vessel fails to understand
the intentions or actions of another.

25
The sound signal made
in restricted visibility by:
• A vessel not under command
• A vessel restricted in its ability to
manoeuvre
• A vessel constrained by its draught
• A sailing vessel
• A vessel engaged in fishing
• A vessel engaged in towing or pushing

It is made every 2 minutes.

28
The sound signal made
when in sight of another vessel.
It means 'I am operating
astern propulsion'.

27
The sound signal made
when in sight of another vessel in
a narrow channel or fairway.
It means 'I intend to overtake
you on your port side'.

30
The sound signal made
in restricted visibility by
a power driven vessel making
way through the water.

It is made every 2 minutes.

29
The sound signal made
in restricted visibility by
a vessel at anchor, giving warning
of her position and of the possibility
of collision with another vessel.

31

Sound Signal

5 seconds
every minute.

32

Sound Signal

3 distinct rings,
5 seconds
continuous ringing,
3 distinct rings,
every minute.

33

Sound Signal

3 distinct rings,
5 seconds
continuous ringing,
3 distinct rings,
5 seconds on
a gong aft,
every minute.

34

Sound Signal

5 seconds ringing of
a bell forward,
5 seconds on
a gong aft,
every minute.

35

Sound Signal

36

Sound Signal

Good visibility?
Restricted visibility?

37

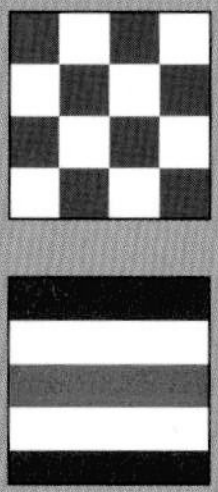

38

32
The sound signal made
in restricted visibility by
a vessel that is less than 100 metres in
length, when aground.

It is made every minute.

31
The sound signal made
in restricted visibility by
a vessel at anchor that is
less than 100 metres in length.

It is made every minute.

34
The sound signal made
in reduced visibility
by a vessel at anchor,
over 100 metres in length.

33
The sound signal made
in restricted visibility by
a vessel that is more than 100 metres
in length, when aground.

It is made every minute.

36
In good visibility by
a vessel nearing
a bend in a channel or fairway
to indicate its presence.

In restricted visibility by
a power driven vessel making way
through the water.

It is made every 2 minutes.

35
The sound signal made
when in sight of another vessel.
It means 'I am altering
my course to port'.

38
The flag hoist
'ROMEO YANKEE'
flown beneath the Answer Pennant.

Meaning:
'Please proceed past me slowly'.

37
The flag hoist
'NOVEMBER CHARLIE'
used by a vessel in distress.

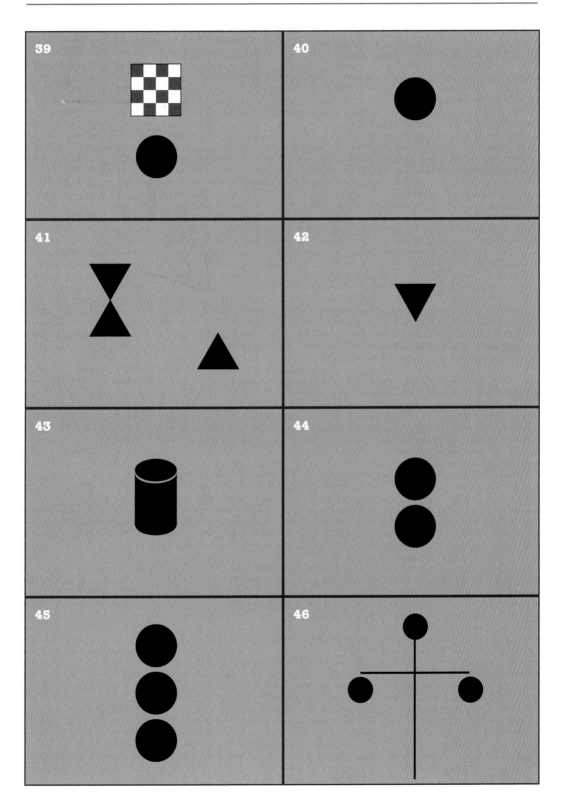

40
The shape hoisted by
a vessel at anchor.

39
A distress signal:

Any square flag flown above
or below a ball or anything
resembling a ball.

42
The shape shown by
a vessel proceeding under
sail when also being
propelled by machinery.

41
The shapes shown by
a vessel engaged in fishing
(other than trawling) with gear
extending more than 150 metres
horizontally from the vessel.

44
The shape shown by
a vessel not under command.

43
The shape shown by
a vessel constrained by its draught.

46
The shape shown by
a vessel engaged in
mineclearance operations.

45
The shape shown by
a vessel aground
(longer than 12 metres).

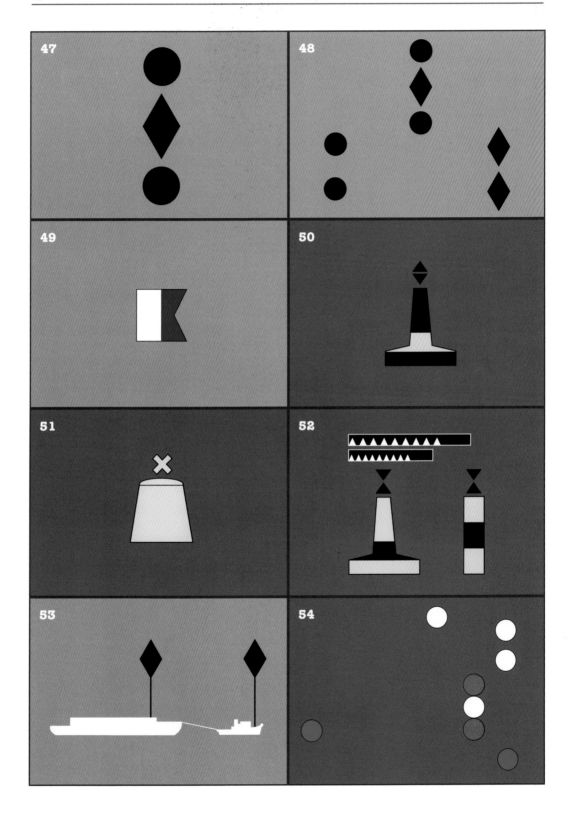

48
The shape shown by
a vessel restricted in its ability
to manoeuvre, engaged in
dredging or underwater operations
with an obstruction on the left
(as we look at it)
and clear on the right.

47
The shape shown by
a vessel restricted in its
ability to manoeuvre.

50
An easterly cardinal buoy.

49
The shape shown by
a vessel engaged in diving
operations. (The vessel being
too small to carry the shapes.)

52
A westerly cardinal buoy.

51
A special mark buoy.

54
Lights of
a tug and single tow
seen from the starboard beam.
The tug and tow are restricted in their
ability to manoeuvre.

53
The shapes carried by a
tug and its tow when the length
of the tow is greater than
200 metres.

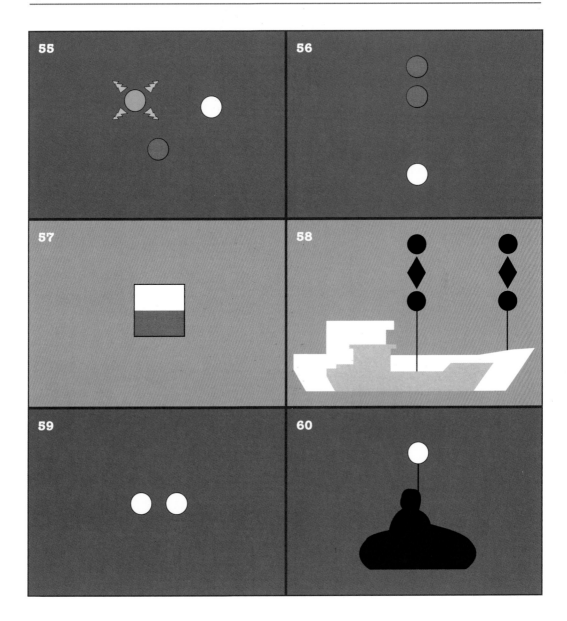

56
The lights of
a vessel not under command
making way, seen from astern.

Could also be a vessel aground less than
50 metres in length, or of more than
50 metres in length when the other anchor
light is obscured by superstructure.

55
The lights of
a police boat or lifeboat on duty
seen from the port side.

58
The shapes shown
by two vessels, restricted in
their ability to manoeuvre,
engaged in replenishment at sea.

57
The flag flown by
a pilot vessel on duty.

60
The lights shown by
a power driven vessel,
less than 7 metres in length
and capable of less than 7 knots.

59
The lights shown by
a tug and tow when
towing alongside,
viewed from astern.